What people are saying about Robert

Angels on the Night Shift

"Excellent book. I read it in one evening. I had a fellow ER nurse borrow it as soon as I finished…Thank you for sharing this book with us."

Ginger

"Fast-paced, fascinating, well-written, and absorbing…I thoroughly enjoyed this and will certainly be looking out for any other books written by this medical author."

TheGardenWindow.blogspot.com

"I love your books! Always wondering who will burst through those doors next! Some of the stories are heartbreaking, some are encouraging, but all of them motivate me to become the best nurse possible. I can't wait for the next one!"

Ruth

Angels and Heroes

"Just wanted to say how much I am enjoying your books…as educational as well as inspirational respites from the day-to-day responsibilities of life… May God bless and keep you."

Kim

"I am not one who likes to read, but when I started I could not put this book down…It made me realize that there are still good people on earth. I am a full-time police officer and a volunteer firefighter/EMS. I can't wait to pass this book on to others in my field."

Gary

"What stories are held in this book—people who just go the whole way to be a help and sacrifice their lives! I am not much of a reader of nonfiction like this…but I fell in love with this book."

GiveawayGal.blogspot.com

Angels on Call

"Thank you for the *amazingly awesome* books you have written. As a Christian pursuing a career in medicine, I find them really inspiring. I had tears in my eyes many times, especially in *Angels on Call.* I love, love, love these books!"

Alina

"As an assistant principal...I have reflected on my own life's work with adolescent students as I read each account...I am writing to share how very much I enjoyed your book, especially the inspiring scriptural references accompanying each story."

Don

"The book was an inspiration during a difficult time in our lives...Your humility and humanity jumped out at me. I truly believe God works through us and that there are angels among us."

Chuck

Angels in the ER

"The most inspiring and relatable book I have read throughout my college career in nursing school...I often feel that my small contributions of extra time with patients or a simple smile have no impact on anyone's life. I was inspired by your book and appreciated the Bible verses throughout."

Katie

"I am a busy working mother but managed to read the entire book in less than three days. The way you described the people and the situations was brilliant...You see things in a very special way and have made me see...thank you."

Jamie

"Having spent ten years as a coordinator for our emergency department, I was very intrigued to read your stories...You have a very eloquent way of relating things that most people will never experience, but probably should... Your kindness, care, and compassion shine through."

Alicia

NOTES
from a
DOCTOR'S POCKET

Robert D. Lesslie, MD

HARVEST HOUSE PUBLISHERS
EUGENE, OREGON

Cover by Left Coast Design, Portland, Oregon

Cover photo © Yuri Arcurs / Shutterstock

All the incidents described in this book are true. Where individuals may be identifiable, they have granted the author and the publisher the right to use their names, stories, and/or facts of their lives in all manners, including composite or altered representations. In all other cases, names, circumstances, descriptions, and details have been changed to render individuals unidentifiable.

NOTES FROM A DOCTOR'S POCKET
Copyright © 2013 by Robert D. Lesslie, MD
Published by Harvest House Publishers
Eugene, Oregon 97402
www.harvesthousepublishers.com

Library of Congress Cataloging-in-Publication Data
    Lesslie, Robert D.
    [Notes. Selections]
    Notes from a doctor's pocket / Robert D. Lesslie, MD.
        pages cm
    ISBN 978-0-7369-5480-8 (pbk.)
    ISBN 978-0-7369-5481-5 (eBook)
    1. Physicians—Anecdotes. 2. Medicine—Anecdotes. I. Title.
    R705.L47 2013
    610.92—dc23

                                                        2013006903

Printed in the United States of America

13 14 15 16 17 18 19 20 21 / BP-JH / 10 9 8 7 6 5 4 3 2 1

*This collection of reflections is dedicated to
the memory of my father,
Thomas Ellis Lesslie,
who taught me the importance of observation
and to not take myself too seriously.*

Acknowledgments

I would espcially like to thank my friends at Harvest House for continuing to believe in my writing; and Barbara, my wife of forty years— the love of my life and my best and worst critic.

Contents

LAYOUT OF THE ER

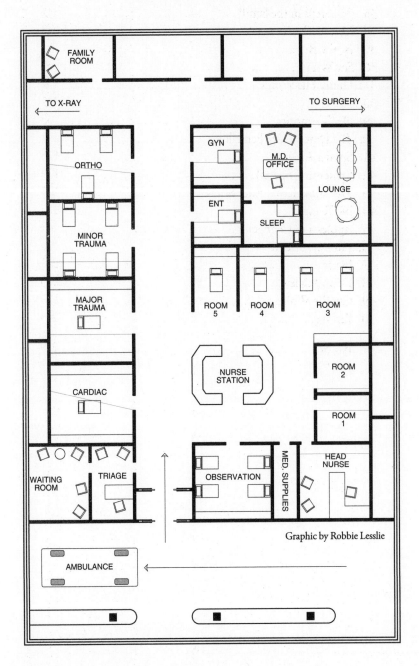

Graphic by Robbie Lesslie

Here, Take a Look at This...

M y wife handed me a tattered piece of paper, smooth from years of wear. Carefully, I unfolded it and began to read the faded note, written long ago in pencil with a halting but elegant hand.

"It's from my grandmother—my daddy's mother," she said. "I found it in Daddy's Bible, just like I bet he found it in hers. Tell me what you think."

She sat down beside me and looked down at the treasure I held in my hands.

Even tho' the night be dark in the valley,
just beyond is shining one eternal light.

I had never met this woman, but knew she was a lady of great faith, one who truly walked with the Lord and loved him mightily. This must have been written in her later years, when her health was fading, and when the night in the valley was becoming dark.

"This is special," I told Barbara, gingerly handing the yellowed note back to her. "We need to keep it in a safe place."

"We need to keep it where we can *read* it," she gently corrected me.

I began to think about that note and about the small bits of paper I had collected over the years. Each had been scribbled and crammed into one or another of my pockets, a way of reminding me of something or someone who was important—something that had struck me as worth remembering. They found their way into a folder somewhere, or an envelope—or tucked into my Bible, just like this one.

This started my search for these slips of paper, for the hastily written word or phrase that had meant a lot to me at some point. And then I began to ask my friends and family if they did the same thing. Thankfully, they did. And before very long, I had a stack of multicolored slips of paper, church bulletins with sermon titles underlined, even high-school graduation programs with quotations scrawled across the top. I had dozens and dozens of pieces of wisdom, treasured and personal thoughts—rare glimpses into the hearts of the people I know and love best.

In these pages are some of those "notes" and the stories that go with them. In them, I hope you will find encouragement, insight, and peace.

We read to know we are not alone.

C.S. LEWIS

1

The Fount of Every Blessing

Mildred Flanders was still in the cardiac room. We were waiting for someone from the ICU to come down and take her upstairs.

We had done all we could, which was precious little for this ninety-two-year-old woman. She had suffered a major stroke sometime during the night and had been found unresponsive by the nursing home staff. It was just going to be a matter of time.

"Call her Millie," one of her attendants had told us. "She never wanted to be called Mildred."

I think I had met Millie years ago, but didn't really know her. However, one of our nurses, Lori Davidson, knew her well. Millie Flanders had taught her in third grade and had been her Sunday-school teacher all through high school.

"That woman knew her Bible," Lori told us. "And she expected us to know it too. And boy could she pray. It was as if the Lord was sitting in the room right beside her and she was carrying on a conversation with him. It was like everything unimportant disappeared and it was just Millie talking with God. It was…it was the way prayer is supposed to be."

Lori and I were the only ones at the nursing station.

"I know no one's perfect," she went on. "But Millie Flanders knows the Lord, and he knows her. And he most definitely answers her prayers."

I glanced over at Lori and our eyes met. Then she tilted her head in the direction of cardiac. Our triage nurse was leading a middle-aged man into the room, and the door was closing behind them.

"What do you mean?" I asked her.

"That's her son," she answered. "Go ask *him*."

The triage nurse was coming out of the room as I entered. Millie was still resting quietly on the stretcher, her eyes closed and her face reflecting a comfortable and transparent peace. On the other side of the bed stood our nurse, making some notes on the chart sitting on the countertop. She looked over at me and then her eyes shifted to the man standing beside the stretcher.

He was well-dressed, lean, and tall, and didn't look up as I walked over beside him. He was gazing at the woman before him, and held her pale, slender hands in his own.

"I'm Dr. Lesslie," I said. "I've been taking care of Mrs. Flanders."

He straightened a little and looked over at me, but didn't release Millie's hands.

"I'm Wes Flanders," he told me. "This is my momma."

I nodded and was about to speak when he said, "I'm her felon."

What did he say?

The comment caught me off guard and my brow furrowed.

"I'm her felon," he repeated, leaning close to me and smiling.

"Okay," I said slowly, not knowing how to respond.

"Do you know Millie?" he asked, tilting his head a little toward his mother.

"Not really," I said. "But some of our staff does. And they think a lot of her."

"She's quite a woman," Wes replied, nodding. "I've put her through a lot. Through a lot she didn't deserve."

I studied his face now, looking for some sign of sadness or grief. After all, his mother was lying in front of him, dying. Instead, there was a warm and tangible serenity about him, and his eyes were soft and kind.

"I haven't been the easiest of sons," he began. "Momma did everything she could for me and was always there, always encouraging and helping me. But I was all about doing my own thing. As I said, I am her felon."

Okay, that was it. He misbehaved when he was younger, and this felon business is an overstatement, hyperbole.

"I was running with the wrong crowd," he continued. "We were into alcohol and drugs. And then things got more serious. We were breaking into houses and stores, and finally I got busted. Grand larceny. All of my 'friends' suddenly didn't know me and they disappeared. I spent three years in prison."

He was still studying my face. I tried to remain unmoved by this revelation. But it was difficult. Here he stood, a man maybe 50 years old, well-spoken and well-dressed, and he was...he was a felon. I had seen and heard a lot worse, but the story and the man in front of me didn't match.

"All of that changed," he told me. "And all because of my momma." He looked down and gently pressed Millie's hands a little tighter.

"I had never been interested in her stories of Jesus. Never paid much attention to her faith or really tried to understand it. I guess some of it must have been sinking in though, because when she—"

He stopped and reached inside his coat pocket, and took out a folded and worn sheet of paper.

"While I was in prison, she visited me almost every day. Wore herself out driving back and forth to Columbia. I told her not to, that she didn't have to do that, but she just shook her head and didn't say anything. And she'd be back the next day. And every day she would pray for me."

He carefully unfolded the paper and cradled it gently in his hand.

"I had been there about two weeks when she gave me this. It's the words to her favorite hymn—'Come, Thou Fount of Every Blessing.' She told me I had to read it every day. And she expected me to memorize it."

He sighed and looked down at Millie, then shook his head.

"I thought she was crazy, and I told her so. But she just smiled at me and said, 'Every day, son. Every day.' Well, I did. And before very long, I had it just about memorized. She had told me to pay special attention to the second verse, to put it in my heart. She said when I understood it, I would be free."

He held the paper up in front of me, making sure I could see it.

"After a while things began to change, and I knew my heart was changing."

I looked down at the faded handwritten words. Someone had circled the second verse and underscored one of the lines.

> _Jesus sought me when a stranger,_
> _Wandering from the fold of God;_
> _He, to rescue me from danger,_
> _Interposed his precious blood._

"Momma was right, Doc. And the Lord answered her prayers. He rescued me and set me free."

Wes Flanders took a deep breath, folded the paper, and slipped it back into his jacket.

Tears were trailing down his cheeks now, and his voice had grown husky.

"She always told me I was her biggest blessing. Me, her felon."

He paused and looked over at me. "But Doc, *she* was *mine*."

Streams of mercy, never ceasing,
Call for songs of loudest praise.

2

A Child's Courage

I can't take it anymore!"

The screaming was coming from minor trauma, and I could hear it all the way in the medicine room. It was the voice of an adult male, obviously upset about something.

"Get away from me!"

I finished washing my hands and stepped out into the ER.

"What in the world?" I said, looking over at Amy Connors. She sat at her desk, shaking her head.

"Arrrgh!"

This outburst caused a couple of curious heads to peep out from the curtains of rooms 2, 3, and 4.

It also caused Virginia Granger to step out of her office and walk over to the nurses' station.

"It's okay," she said to the gaping patients and family members. "Just go back into your rooms. Everything will be fine. There's nothing to worry about."

She looked over at me and shook her head. Then with an unmistakable frown and nod, she silently instructed me to go find out what was going on.

As I walked down the hallway I heard the metal rings of curtains being drawn closed. It seemed that even strangers knew to obey the directives of Virginia Granger.

Just as I turned to enter the room, there was another outburst.

"Argh! You're killing me!"

My eyes were immediately drawn to the bed in the back left corner. There sat a slender eighty-year-old man huddled against the wall, wide-eyed, with his knees drawn to his chest. He had come in a half hour earlier after twisting his ankle, and we were waiting on an X-ray. He frantically looked at me and then at the commotion in the stretcher across from him.

There stood Cindy Jamison, one of our first-shift nurses. She looked over at me, her faced flushed and clouded with frustration. She tried without success to blow a wayward strand of hair from her forehead. In each of her gloved hands she held some pieces of 4x4 gauze.

Before her, sitting on the stretcher, was the source of the hullabaloo. Ty Higgins was forty-two years old and a giant of a man. He towered over most people at six feet, eight inches, and weighed a muscular three hundred, at least.

"Doctor, make her stop!" he cried out pleading when he saw me enter the room.

I turned again to the elderly man in the corner, walked over, and pulled the curtain around his stretcher.

"Everything's okay," I told him quietly. "We'll be getting you around to X-ray in just a few minutes."

He just stared at me, wide-eyed and slack-jawed.

Then I turned back to Ty Higgins and walked over to his stretcher.

"What's the problem here?" I asked Cindy, looking first at her and then down at Higgins.

"Mr. Higgins here has a burn of his—" She had barely begun before he interrupted.

"I burned my hand with hot coffee!" he bellowed, holding up the injured extremity. It was wrapped with a kitchen towel that seemed to have been soaked in water. "It hurts like heck! And this nurse," he grumbled, tossing his head in Cindy's direction, "is about as gentle as a…a… an ox!"

Cindy smiled a little at this and held on to her gauze, patiently waiting.

"She was trying to pull my towel off and it was killing me!" Ty went on.

"We just need to take a look at the burn and get it cleaned up," she patiently explained.

"You were trying to *kill* me!" he exploded again.

"Hold on a minute," I said, stepping closer to the bed. "Cindy's right. We need to take a look at this."

Then reaching out and gently holding his gigantic forearm in one hand, I grasped a loose corner of the wet towel.

"I'm going to take this off so I can see. Okay?"

Higgins looked down at his hand and slowly nodded his head.

"Just be careful, please," he mumbled, his voice suddenly high-pitched and trembling.

The towel came off with ease—and with barely a whimper.

"Hmm…" Cindy murmured.

"What's the matter?" he exclaimed, looking back and forth from Cindy to me. "How bad is it?"

Then he turned his head away, facing the wall.

"Tell me, Doc. How bad is it?"

I glanced up at Cindy and shook my head. The back of Ty Higgins's hand was a little reddened, a pale rose color. No blisters. No evidence of any significant burn. I carefully rolled it over and examined his palm. Nothing.

"Tell me, Doc," he said again, still staring at the wall. "How bad is it?"

I explained that a burn sometimes took twenty-four hours to "declare itself." Cindy would need to gently clean and dress the wound—stressing the word *gently*—and then his family doctor would need to check it in the morning to be sure it hadn't gotten worse.

"Thanks, Doc," he muttered, still not looking down at his hand. "Thanks."

I walked back to the nurses' station and the waiting Virginia Granger.

"Everything okay back there?" she asked.

"Done," I told her, chuckling. "Shouldn't be any more disturbance coming from minor trauma."

"Good," she replied, sliding the chart of room 4 over to me. "Jimmy Evans is here, and his mother wants you to see him."

I looked down at the clipboard and took a deep breath, my emotions abruptly spinning in a different direction.

Jimmy Evans was a seven-year-old boy I had first met in the ER a little over a year ago. His parents had brought him in because of a low-grade fever, fatigue, and some strange bruises on his back and arms. A few lab tests later and we had our answer. Jimmy had an aggressive form of leukemia, and he needed urgent treatment.

His parents had taken him to a highly regarded cancer center and he had responded remarkably well. Within a few months he was in remission and back in school, and to any stranger's eye was a typical young boy.

That changed when he came into the ER a month or two later with a nosebleed that wouldn't stop. His platelets had dropped dangerously low, and soon he was back in treatment. This time his response was slower, and the doctors' prognosis was more guarded. He would occasionally need blood transfusions—we had arranged to have them done here in the ER.

That must be why he's here. He needs another transfusion.

I picked up his chart and walked over to room 4. As I pulled the curtain open, a lab tech stepped out, holding her wire-mesh basket of supplies in one hand and a tube of blood in the other.

"Type and cross for two units," she told me, passing by quickly and heading to the lab.

Jimmy's mother was standing by the stretcher, her back to me. She was gently rubbing his shoulder as I walked over.

"Hey, Dr. Lesslie," she said cheerfully, turning to face me. "I'm glad you could see us."

"Hey, Doc," Jimmy echoed.

He was sitting on the stretcher with his legs sprawled out in front of him, dressed in blue pajamas and wearing some kind of animal-shaped slippers.

"Whatcha think?" he asked, smiling and rubbing his completely bald head. His eyebrows were gone as well. He had lost his hair since I had last seen him and it was a shock.

"I like it," I told him, reaching over and rubbing his head. "Won't need a brush for a while, will you?"

"I like it too," he grinned. "Makes me look like Grandpa."

We talked a while about what needed to happen and how long they would be in the ER. They were old hands at this, but I wanted to be sure they knew what to expect.

"How about this hand?" he asked, holding up his left arm. "They used my right one last time."

I glanced over at his mother. She still had her hand on her boy's shoulder and was gazing down at him. She was smiling, but her lip was trembling just a little.

"I'll be sure to tell the nurse," I told him, turning to the doorway. "You're a brave young man, Mr. Evans."

His mother was nodding silently as I left the room.

Coming down the hallway was Ty Higgins, his bandaged hand raised high in the air. Our eyes met just as he turned into the triage hallway. He was shaking his head and his lips formed a silent "oooo."

I just stood and stared at him. And was thankful for Jimmy Evans.

Courage doesn't always roar...

MARY ANNE RADMACHER (1957–)

3

WOLVES IN SHEEP'S CLOTHING

A nything to turn over?" Liz Kennick asked.
I looked up from a chart and over to my partner. She was my relief tonight, and I was glad to see her. The last few hours had been hectic.

"No, this is my last patient," I told her. "But it looks like you're going to be busy for a while."

She glanced around the chaotic department and nodded her head.

"We'll get it under control."

She looked down at the unit secretary and said, "I'm going to drop some stuff in our office and be right back."

She turned and started down the hallway, then tossed a quick farewell over her shoulder—"See you in the morning, Robert."

Liz had finished her emergency medicine residency a little over six months ago and had joined us right after that. She was going to be a good ER doc. She already possessed the necessary skills and education. What she lacked in experience would come with time.

The next morning as I walked through the parking lot on my way to the ER, I noticed an elderly patient exiting the hospital in a wheelchair. He was slumped over and being pushed by two women dressed in nurses' outfits. For some reason I stopped and watched as they rolled the chair up to a van, slid the side door open, and roughly lifted the old man up and into the vehicle. The door closed, and in the early morning light I could just make out "Green Valley Retirement Village."

As they pulled out, I again headed toward the entrance.

Liz was standing at the nurses' station, bag in hand, waiting for me.

"Everything's clear," she told me, her cheerful voice belying the fatigue etched on her face. "Not too bad a night."

"Tell me about the man in the wheelchair," I asked her, curious. "The one that just left."

"Hmm, oh, Mr. Clives," she answered, slowly nodding her head.

"Some of the staff from Green Valley brought him in a little while ago with a low-grade fever. Urinary tract infection was all we found. Gave him a shot of Rocephin and a couple of prescriptions and sent him back," she said matter-of-factly. "He's almost ninety years old. Had a stroke a few years ago and can't talk, but he seemed to be okay."

She had turned to leave, but suddenly stopped and faced me again. "Why?"

"I don't know," I told her. "Just saw him out in the parking lot and…I was curious."

"Well, he's doing pretty well to be as old as he is, and the staff there seems to be taking good care of him."

This time she didn't stop, and soon disappeared through the exit.

Two weeks later Liz and I were working together during a day shift. The morning had crescendoed into a busy afternoon, and at a little after three we were both at the nurses' station, trying to catch our breath.

The triage nurse put the chart of minor trauma B on the counter, then disappeared.

Liz looked down at it and remarked, "Mr. Clives is here again. Remember, the ninety-year-old from the nursing center?"

A lot of patients came through the department, but I remembered Mr. Clives.

"Let's see," she mused, scanning the record. "Lacerations of his left arm. I'll take care of that."

She headed down the hallway, and I finished writing up a couple of charts. A few minutes later Liz walked back up and said, "Poor man. He has 'onion skin'—you know, paper-thin, and it tears so easily. His whole forearm is shredded. Apparently he slipped out of his chair and fell against the edge of his bed. His nurses back there are so worried about him. I told them it just happens, and it doesn't take much to rip his skin."

She started making notes then started mumbling to herself. "I'll just glue it back together, I suppose. Sure can't put any sutures in it."

"You say his nurses are back there with him?" I asked.

"Yeah, they brought him over from Green Valley—two of them—and they haven't left his side. Like I said, they're really worried about him."

"How is he acting?" I asked. "I mean, how is he responding, to you and to his nurses?"

She stopped writing and looked up at me. Her brow furrowed and she tapped her chin with her pen.

"He can't talk, you remember, but he seems to be okay. He seems to be aware of what's going on and doesn't act like he's in any pain. Why?"

"I don't know really. Just a—"

"Dr. Lesslie," the unit secretary interrupted. "The neurosurgeon is on the line for you."

She was handing me the phone and I turned to Liz.

"I need to get this."

"Sure," she said, then picked up the clipboard for Mr. Clives and walked down the hall.

One thing quickly led to another, and before I could get back to check on this elderly patient, he was gone and on his way back to Green Valley.

Three weeks later Mr. Clives was brought in by ambulance. He had fallen again, and the staff at Green Valley thought he might have broken his left hip.

So did the paramedics, and they had placed him in traction and on a long backboard.

It was seven p.m., shift change, and I was just coming on duty. Liz Kennick was headed out the ambulance entrance, when the stretcher with Mr. Clives rolled through. She looked down, recognized him, and did an about-face.

"What's going on here?" she asked the paramedics.

"Looks like a broken hip," one of them told her, pausing briefly and then heading again into the department.

"Ortho," Jeff Ryan called over to them from just outside the medicine room. "Bed 1."

"How did it happen?" Liz asked the two attendants following the paramedics. She recognized the Green Valley nurses from the previous visit.

"He tripped and—" one began before being quickly interrupted by her partner.

"He *slipped* out of his wheelchair this evening. We're not sure how he fell—it just happened so fast."

I had heard all of this and was already headed down the hallway after his stretcher.

"Amy, be sure those two go out to the waiting room," I told the secretary, pointing to the two nurses. "I don't want them back here."

She jumped up from her chair and was around the counter before the nurses could follow me. Over their protestations Amy guided them through triage and out to the waiting room.

Liz was right behind me as I walked into ortho.

"Hold on," I told the paramedics. "Let me take a look at Mr. Clives."

Liz was at my shoulder, looking down at our patient. His eyes darted back and forth from her face to mine, his face riddled with pain—and with fear.

I spoke quietly to him and examined his injured hip. It was fractured, and he would need surgery to repair it. I told him that, then gently began to examine his chest. He grimaced as I did this, and with only a little pressure I could feel the grating of fractured ribs.

"Did this happen when you fell?" I asked him softly.

He shook his head and his eyes widened. He was struggling to speak, his mouth moving wordlessly.

"This wasn't an accident, was it?" I asked him.

I could see Liz tense as he shook his head again. He raised his head from the backboard and began looking around the room, around and behind us.

"They're not here," I told him. "And they won't be. You won't have to worry about them anymore."

His head fell back on the thin pillow and he closed his eyes.

"What—" Liz began.

"Not now," I stopped her. "But would you go tell Amy to get lab down here, get ortho on the phone, and notify the OR?"

"Sure," she answered, turning to the doorway.

I was shaking with anger as I said, "And tell her to call the police."

My doctrine is this,
that if we see cruelty or wrong that we have the power to stop,
and do nothing,
we make ourselves sharers in the guilt.

ANNA SEWELL (1820–1878)

4

A Doubled Grief

The ambu bag was getting harder to squeeze. That meant we didn't have much time. Jason's lungs were getting stiffer and harder to ventilate.

"Any pulse?" I asked Jeff Ryan. He was standing by the stretcher with his fingers on the six-year-old's femoral artery.

"Nothing," he answered, shaking his head and glancing over at the cardiac monitor. "Still flatline."

Lori hurried back into the room and came over to where I stood.

"Here are his labs," she said, holding a slip of paper where I could read the list of numbers. Nothing was normal. His electrolytes were all out of whack.

I turned to the two people standing in the corner of the room.

"How long do you think he was in the pool?" I asked.

They looked at each other and then Jason's mother turned to me. "It couldn't have been more than five...maybe six minutes."

Her voice was cracking and then she broke into sobs.

"He was in the kitchen with us," Jason's father took over. "And then he was gone, outside. We didn't even...I didn't even know he had left the room..."

"That's okay," I said quietly, turning again to the boy in front of me.

Five or six minutes. That was a long time for him to be underwater.

I looked over at the wall clock. We had been working with him for over an hour—nothing. His pupils were dilated and he had no pulse or cardiac activity.

Lori met my glance, her large brown eyes blinking rapidly as she tried to fight back the tears. Her chin trembled as she nodded her head.

It was time, and I knew it.

I glanced again at the couple in the corner. They were standing with their arms around each other, she with her head down, and he with his eyes fixed on mine. I shook my head slowly. His eyes widened and he clutched his wife even tighter.

"Lori, we need to call it," I told her, disconnecting the ambu bag and placing it on the stretcher beside the lifeless boy.

There was a faint wheezing as the last traces of air escaped from his lungs.

She sighed heavily, glanced over at the clock, and said, "Four-fifty-two."

Everything stopped, and for a moment we all just stood there. Then slowly Jason's mother and father walked over to the stretcher, still with their arms around each other.

"I'm sorry," I told them. "We did everything we could."

"We know you did, Dr. Lesslie," the father said, his voice trembling. "We know you did."

Slowly Jason's mother reached out and brushed back the hair from her boy's forehead. Then she collapsed on the stretcher, hugging her young son. Long, painful sobs filled the room. I had to leave.

An hour later Lori came up to me at the nurses' station.

"Jason's relatives are back in the family room," she told me. "There are a lot of them. Aunts and uncles, grandparents. Do you need some help?"

It was a small room, and that sounded like a crowd of people. As much as I wanted her back there with me, I said, "No, I can handle it."

The room *was* crowded, with barely a place for me to stand. Jason's parents were sitting on the small sofa, holding hands and leaning closely into each other. A man about Jason's father's age stood beside the father, his hand on the grieving man's shoulder.

"I'm Jason's uncle," he told me. "And these—" he waved his arm expansively, "we're all family."

I quickly scanned the room, silently nodding my head. Crowded into a corner stood an elderly couple, huddled closely together, their heads bowed.

I looked back at the brother and then down at the parents.

"I'll be glad to answer any questions you might have," I told them. "Anything that might be on your heart right now."

An awkward silence followed, broken only by an occasional sob. Jason's parents hung their heads and didn't say anything. I needed to.

"We couldn't save Jason," I told them. "And I'm sorry. But this was no one's fault. It happened, and it's hard."

I heard my own voice trembling and I struggled for the next words.

"I want you two to hear that, okay?" I said, looking down at his parents.

Jason's father looked up at me, his eyes red and filled with tears. He nodded his head.

"This was not your fault," I repeated. "And tomorrow, and the day after, and ten years from now, I want you to remember that. It was not your fault."

I couldn't give them their son back, but I desperately wanted to give them what little peace I could. And I knew the burden of guilt was an awful and heavy weight.

I stood there for another minute or so as the family gathered around the two on the sofa. I glanced again at the couple in the corner. They tried to join the group around the parents, but there was no room.

Twenty minutes later I walked into the medicine room to get some supplies for a patient in minor trauma. Lori was standing at the window, staring into the parking lot, her shoulders slumped.

"That's always hard, isn't it?" she sighed.

I knew she was talking about Jason and his parents.

"Yeah, it's always hard. But they seem to be a close family, and that will help them."

"I know," she said quietly. "But I'm worried about those two."

I glanced over at her. "You mean his parents?"

"No," she said. "*Those* two." She nodded her head in the direction of the ER parking lot.

I stepped over and looked out the window.

It was the elderly couple from back in the family room—the two huddled in the corner. They were slowly making their way across the parking lot, alone, with their arms around each other.

"I think if it's possible," Lori said quietly, "it might be the hardest on grandparents. They have a different kind of love. Not only do they grieve the loss of their grandchild, but they grieve for their *child* and *their* loss. I can't imagine the pain."

I glanced down at her and then back out into the parking lot. The elderly man was opening the door of the car for his wife. After she got in, he closed it and just stood there, staring down at the pavement.

"And you know," Lori spoke again. "Sometimes I think we forget about them, and about their pain."

The image of them standing alone in the corner returned to me, and the image of their futile effort to join their grieving children. My heart sank. *What should I have done? What could I have done?*

"I just hope they're not forgotten," Lori whispered.

*Perfect love sometimes does not come
until the first grandchild.*

WELSH PROVERB

NEVER ENOUGH

3:00 a.m. Sam Young was an internal medicine specialist and one of the most highly regarded of the teaching faculty at the hospital. He took special care of his patients, and was always willing to come in and help when we needed him in the ER. Just like tonight.

"Well, that should just about do it," he said to me, signing the admission orders for an elderly woman whose diabetes had gotten out of control.

We were sitting behind the nurses' station, and when he slid the chart over to the secretary, instead of standing up to head back home, he folded his hands behind his head, leaned back in his chair, and asked, "Robert, how are things going?"

He was looking at me intently, and I wasn't sure how to answer this question. I was a resident rotating through the emergency department—was he asking about my work in the ER? About my decision to pursue a career in emergency medicine? Something about my personal life?

When I hesitated, he took a deep breath, exhaled loudly, and began.

"I know it's tough being a resident. Tough to make ends meet with the amount of money you guys and gals get paid."

He was right about that, but it was the price we needed to pay to complete our training. It wouldn't always be this way.

"Just be careful," he cautioned me.

"What do you mean?" I asked, becoming curious.

"Well, money will always be a temptation, and a challenge," he explained. "And one of the most important lessons you can learn is that no matter how much you make, or how little, most of us will find some way to live at the very edge. There's never enough, or so it seems. And it's not hard to fall over that edge."

He gave me a minute for that to sink in, then added, "And remember this—the more things you own, the more things own you. I'm speaking from experience, Robert. If you can avoid some of those traps, you will have learned something. And you'll save yourself a lot of grief and wasted time. Maybe wasted years."

He was looking beyond me now, lost in his own thoughts. I sat there quietly, considering all he had just told me.

With a deep sigh, he stood up to leave. Turning back to me he said, "My wife and I are having a mortgage-burning party next weekend. Finally paid the house off, and we want some of you residents to come, if you can. Bring your wife—it should be a good time."

He walked out of the department and I sat there, thinking.

The more things you own, the more things own you. I wanted to be sure those words were forever seared in my mind and heart.

The mortgage burning *was* a good time, and a lot of us residents helped Sam and his family celebrate this financial milestone.

Then, three weeks later at the age of fifty-six, Sam Young was dead of a heart attack.

The ground of a certain rich man
yielded an abundant harvest.
He thought to himself, "What shall I do?
I have no place to store my crops…
This is what I'll do.
I will tear down my barns and build bigger ones…"
But God said to him, "You fool!
This very night your life will be demanded from you.
Then who will get what you have prepared for yourself?"

Luke 12:16-18,20

DEVIL ON MY SHOULDER

I f you looked in a dictionary under *pompous* you would probably find a picture of Theodore Middleton III. And he would probably be proud of it.

Theodore—excuse me—*Dr.* Middleton did some moonlighting in our ER while finishing his residency in dermatology in Columbia. Clinically, he was a solid and capable physician. But he left quite a mark for himself.

So let me explain.

"Amy, we need a chest X-ray on the man in 5," I told our secretary, then slid his chart toward her.

Theodore Middleton III stepped out of room 3, closed the curtain behind him, and joined me at the nurses' station.

He was studying the clipboard in front of him, when Jeff Ryan walked up.

"You think he has shingles?" Jeff asked Middleton, tilting his head in the direction of the room the doctor had just left.

Middleton looked over at Jeff, and the nurse's eyes bulged and his mouth dropped. Amy looked up, put her hand over her own mouth, and quickly turned away. She was shaking, and I wanted to know what was going on.

"You might very well be correct," Theodore responded primly. "It just might be the shingles."

Jeff was still staring at Middleton as the doctor resumed writing on his chart. I looked closely at him and quickly understood.

Theodore paused in his writing, put his pen in the corner of his mouth, and slowly nodded his head up and down. It was a habit he had developed—one we had come to accept. This time, unbeknownst to him, his ballpoint had sprung a leak and a thick black line had dribbled from the corner of his mouth to his chin. He had no clue.

Amy spun back in her chair and said, "Dr. Mid—"

Jeff put his finger to his lips and shook his head vigorously.

"Yes, Mrs. Connors?" the doctor responded, looking up from his work.

Amy was biting her lip, struggling mightily, and finally muttered, "Will you…be needing any…lab work?"

Theodore looked back at room 3 and said, "Not necessary. I have my diagnosis."

And with that he grabbed a prescription pad and walked back into the room.

Amy let out a sigh and shook her head, chuckling.

"Well, I never…"

"Amy, quick!" Jeff said, leaning over the countertop. "Give me a pencil and a piece of copy paper."

"How about a pen?" she responded, holding up her own ballpoint.

"No, it has to be a pencil."

Amy searched in one of the drawers, found a pencil, and handed it to Jeff. She passed him a piece of paper just as Middleton walked back over.

"Strange response," he murmured.

"What do you mean?" I asked, studying the spreading ink stain on his chin.

"Just the way the patient looked at me when I told him he had shingles. Strange, that's all." And with that, he tossed the chart into the discharge basket.

"Dr. Lesslie, I want you to try something," Jeff said, taking the piece of copy paper and placing it carefully on the countertop. Then he drew a quarter-sized circle on it and took a quarter out of his pants pocket.

He leaned over the counter, rolled the quarter up and down his nose and forehead, and then let it fall onto the paper. It came to rest a few inches from the circle.

"Doggone it!" he exclaimed in seeming frustration.

He picked up the quarter and repeated the process, with the same result.

"Doggone it! I don't know how that guy did it."

"Did what?" Theodore Middleton III had been intently watching Jeff's every move, his head tilted to one side.

"One of our paramedics can drop a quarter into that circle every time! It's uncanny! Here, you try, Dr. Lesslie."

"No," Middleton interjected. "Let me have that quarter. This doesn't look so difficult."

He grabbed the quarter and pushed Jeff out of the way, then leaned over the paper. Jeff winked at me and then at Amy.

"Is this about right?" Middleton asked Jeff.

Jeff stepped back a little, looking this way and that at the doctor, then said, "Your head needs to be down just a little. Twelve inches above the paper, no closer."

Middleton made some adjustments and was putting the quarter on his nose, when Jeff said, "Hold on a minute!"

He took the quarter from Middleton, put it on the piece of paper, and started outlining it repeatedly with the pencil.

"The trick is to get more than half of it in the circle," he patiently explained. "And I've never seen anyone land it perfectly, except that paramedic."

"Humph," Middleton muttered impatiently, grabbing the quarter from Jeff.

He put it on his nose when Jeff once again stopped him.

"No, you need to carefully line it up," he instructed. "Up and down, remember?"

"Oh yes," the doctor apologized. He ran the quarter up and down his nose and forehead a few times then let it fall. It came to rest barely on the paper, nowhere near the circle.

"Here, let's try it again," Jeff said, picking up the quarter and again running the pencil around its edges. "Okay, now try."

This went on for several minutes, with each failed attempt followed by Jeff applying a new coating of graphite to the edges of the quarter.

Finally exasperated, Dr. Middleton straightened up and said, "Here, Robert—you try."

Amy took one look at him, coughed loudly, and spun around in her chair. I had to look away.

Theodore stood before us with his immaculate, starched lab coat, his bright-red bow tie, and his perfectly coiffed hair. The same dark ink stain trailed down his chin, and now there was a heavy black line running from his forehead to the tip of his nose.

"No," I managed to say. "If *you* can't do it, I won't even try."

The triage nurse had just put a chart on the countertop. She took one look at Dr. Middleton and hurried away.

"Why don't you see this one," I said, sliding the chart toward Theodore. "I've got to check on my patient back in minor trauma."

"Sure," he said, looking down at the record. "Three-year-old with a sore throat. That should be quick."

Ten minutes later, the three of us were once again standing at the nurses' station.

"Any orders for that patient?" Amy asked Middleton, afraid to look up at him.

"No, just a routine pharyngitis," he answered. "But you know, his mother was strange. Just like the man with shingles. She just looked at me and stared. And the child! You would have thought he had seen a ghost."

Amy snorted and turned away, just as Virginia Granger walked up.

She took one look at Theodore and then at Jeff. Finally she looked over at me and lowered her head, her eyes barely slits by this point—a bull ready to charge.

"Dr. Middleton, would you come with me a moment?"

She spun on her heels and headed into the medicine room. Theodore turned and followed her.

Jeff, Amy, and I looked at each other, grinning and waiting.

And then we heard it.

"What the—!"

I generally avoid temptation
unless I can't resist it.

Mae West (1892–1980)

7

Are You Standing Your Ground or Turning Around?

Hand me the chest tube!" I called over my shoulder to Lori, who was gloved and standing ready by my side.

"Here," she said, handing me the hollow plastic tubing.

I used the hemostat to enlarge the hole I had made in Sergio's left chest and then slid the tube in, pointing it up toward his neck.

"Okay, you can connect it to the suction bottle," I told her, then took a step back and waited.

As soon as she connected it, the water in the bottle began to bubble angrily, indicating the chest tube was in the right place and working. Then bright red blood began flowing into the container.

"Is he going to be okay, Doc?"

I looked over to the corner where a police officer and detective were standing. The officer looked a little pale, and I pointed to a nearby chair. He averted his eyes from my patient's chest and stumbled over, sitting down awkwardly.

Looking back at the detective I said, "The bullet missed his heart, but it collapsed his lung and must have hit a vessel. He'll need surgery and then we'll see."

"100 over 60," Jeff called out.

Good. His pressure was coming up.

"Is the thoracic surgeon on his way down?" I asked Lori.

"He was in the OR and he knows to come right over," she answered, snapping off her gloves and tossing them into a trash can. "Should be any minute now."

"Just the one gunshot?" the detective asked me.

I was growing a little impatient. I knew he had a job to do—to try to determine who had shot this man and left him in a burning house. But my job was to save his life, and we weren't there yet.

"Just the one—that's all I've seen, Jake," I told him.

"Just one bullet."

The accent was heavy, but the man on the stretcher, Sergio Hernandez, spoke perfect English. I stepped closer and said, "Just the one shot? Are you sure?"

"*Sí*. Yes, Doctor, just the one. I am sure."

He grimaced and shifted a little on the stretcher.

"We can give you something more for pain, if you need it," I told him.

"No, I'm okay," he answered. "But you were right. That hurt a little." The smile was forced as he nodded in the direction of the chest tube.

"I'm sorry about that," I said. "But it needed to be done. And it's helping."

I listened to his chest again, moving the stethoscope from side to side. *Better. And his color was better.*

Then I checked his nose again. There was a little soot around the edges, but his nasal hairs had not been singed. Hopefully there had only been a small amount of smoke inhalation. If not, he would be in big trouble.

It had been a major fire somewhere on Ison Street, in a part of town located near some closed and dilapidated textile mills. The house was almost gone when the fire units got there, with two EMS vehicles close on their heels.

The paramedics had told us they'd found Sergio face down in the yard, just barely out of the house. There was a trail of blood down the steps and over to where he lay.

"I'm not sure how he got out of there," the paramedic told me. "He wasn't talking when we got to him, and didn't have much of a blood pressure. It's a miracle he didn't burn up in that house."

That was the intent, or so the detective thought. Jake was here because it was an attempted homicide. Sergio had been shot in the chest and then the house had been torched.

"Can I talk to him now?" Jake had moved over beside me, his notepad in one hand and a ballpoint pen in the other.

I glanced back at him and then down at Sergio. He nodded.

"Okay, but you've only got a couple of minutes," I told him. "Once the surgeon is here, he'll be on his way to the OR."

Jake asked him a few questions while I continued to examine Sergio's arms and legs. There were some second-degree burns on the backs of his calves. That made sense, if he had been crawling down the steps with flames lapping at him. The paramedic was right—he had just barely made it.

"Did you see the guy who shot you?" Jake was asking.

"Jeremy Hite," Sergio whispered in reply.

"Jeremy Hite?" Jake repeated. His eyes had widened and his voice was higher-pitched. "Are you sure?"

"It was Jeremy Hite."

The door to trauma swung open and the thoracic surgeon walked in.

"What have we got here, Robert?"

After Sergio's stretcher rolled out of the room, I was alone with Jake and the slowly recovering police officer, who was still sitting down. The floor was littered with pieces of paper, bloody gauze, and some gloves that had missed the trash can. I leaned back against the counter, glad for the sudden quiet.

"He'll make it, won't he?" Jake broke the silence, his voice low and less than sure.

"I think so," I told him. "He's healthy, and lucky. That goes a long way."

"He's a good man," Jake said, stretching and beginning to pace the cluttered floor. "He and his family live in a tough part of town, not too far from Ison Street. Used to be a good neighborhood, but like everything else, things change. We got a call from him about two months ago. He had heard there was a meth lab over on Ison, but didn't have the address or any names. Just had heard something was going on, and he was worried about his two teenage kids. Didn't want them getting messed up with any of that. We checked it out, but didn't find anything."

"Somebody had set up shop in an abandoned house," the police officer interjected. "But they must have gotten wind of something, 'cause they'd packed up their stuff and moved on."

Jake, still pacing, nodded and came to a stop in front of me.

"Got another call a couple of weeks ago from Sergio. Same thing. But this time he gave us an address. No names, but he was right. There was stuff still cooking when we got there."

"What do you think happened this time?" I asked him.

Jake stroked his chin and stared down at the floor.

"I think they figured out who was calling the cops and wanted to put a stop to it. I'm not sure how they got Sergio over to that house, or if he somehow found them, but it doesn't matter. They tried to kill him and then cover it up."

"What about this Jeremy Hite guy?" I asked.

"He's a bad actor," the officer spoke up. "Into a lot of stuff here in Rock Hill."

"We've just never been able to nail him with any of it," Jake said. "Not until now. We'll leave here and go pick him up. He'll be surprised to learn Sergio is still alive."

"Let's hope he stays alive," I said quietly. "Sounds like he really put himself in harm's way."

Jake sighed and looked up at me. "He did, Doc. He just wouldn't turn his head and let this pass. You know, we need more people like Sergio, don't we?"

...so that when the day of evil comes,
you may be able to stand your ground,
and after you have done everything,
to stand.

EPHESIANS 6:13

8

THE STRANGER

W hat's the strangest thing you've ever seen in the ER?"
I get asked that a lot. I guess that's true for all of us who work in
the ER. But this time it was my fifteen-year-old daughter asking the question, and I gave it some thought.

Should I tell her about the woman who was convinced she was possessed and tore her tongue out? Or what about the fella who kept a bottle of cheap wine hidden in his wooden leg?

"I guess it depends on what you mean by *strange,*" I temporized.

She sat there for a moment with a serious look on her face.

Finally she said, "I suppose I'd like to hear something that happened out of the clear blue. Something you didn't expect and couldn't explain."

There goes the wooden leg story.

We were driving down the interstate, just the two of us, and I glanced over at her. She sat patiently, looking up at me, waiting.

There *was* a story that I couldn't explain, one that had taken me completely by surprise. And I knew I needed to share it with her.

Jeff Ryan and I were standing in major trauma, and we both heard the ambulance entrance doors open. He looked over at me and nodded. Then he turned to the counter again, making sure he had everything he needed.

EMS 2 had called in a gunshot wound to the thigh—a forty-eight-year-old man with no blood pressure. They had started an IV, loaded him into the ambulance, and headed to the ER with lights flashing and siren blasting. Jeff and I were waiting for them, along with one of the lab techs.

"We'll need to type and cross for four units as soon as you can get to him," I told her. She was snapping her gloves on and nodded without saying anything.

We heard the stretcher wheels clicking as the crew came down the hallway, and then everything broke loose.

The two paramedics were red-faced and spoke hurriedly, interrupting each other.

"Hold on!" I told them as we moved the pale and limp body to the trauma-room bed. "Jerry, tell me what's going on."

"I've never seen so much blood in all my life, Doc," he told me, wiping his bloody hands on the front of his blood-covered trousers. "He can't have much left in him. It's all on the ground back at Veteran's Park."

"Is that where this happened?" Jeff asked while starting another IV.

"Yeah," the paramedic answered. "Veteran's Park."

"What's his name?" I asked. The man's eyelids were partially open—his eyes were glazed, but his pupils reacted a little to my flashlight. That was something.

"Lenny Barker," Jerry answered. "At least that's what somebody who arrived at the scene told us. They said he works at the Salvation Army, right around the corner."

"Lenny!" I shouted in the man's ear. I thought he grimaced just a little, and I quickly glanced over at the heart monitor: 120. Fast, but at least it was regular.

"Any blood pressure?" I asked Jeff.

"I think I hear something around 60, but it's faint. And he has a carotid pulse, but that's weak too."

"Get both lines going wide open," I directed him. Then I turned to the lab tech and said, "Get that blood drawn as fast as you can. And we need six units, not four—and we need it yesterday!"

I grabbed Lenny's shirt and ripped it open, sending buttons flying around the room.

"How many times was he shot?" I asked while feeling his abdomen and examining what I could see of his chest.

"Just the one," Jerry answered. "The right thigh. We got a good look but couldn't find anything else."

"Someone nearby said they only heard one gunshot."

It was Bill Weathers, a sergeant with the city police. He had slipped into the room without my seeing him.

I nodded at him. "Do we know anything else?"

"Just that he was walking in the park alone," Bill answered. "And—"

"What are you doing!" I yelled.

Another nurse had come into the room and was about to cut off what looked like a tourniquet that had been placed around the man's leg.

She jumped back and stared wide-eyed at me.

"Don't touch that!" I told her. "We need to keep that in place until we know what we've got."

She backed away, and out of the corner of my eye I could see Jeff motion for her to step around to his side of the stretcher.

I moved nearer to his wounded leg and took a closer look. The paramedics must have used their scissors to cut his pants leg from the bottom all the way to the groin. His trousers were soaked in blood and his lower leg was drained and white.

"Did you guys put this on?" I asked, gently fingering what appeared to be a scarlet-colored scarf, tied neatly around the man's thigh. I slipped a finger under it, making sure it wasn't on too tight. It had been expertly positioned and was applying just the right amount of pressure.

When they didn't answer, I looked up at Jerry. He glanced over at his partner and then back at me.

"We didn't do it, Doc," he said hesitantly. "It was on when we got there. Whoever put it on knew what they were doing and probably saved this man's life, or at least gave him a chance."

"Who was it?" I asked, looking back down and resuming my examination.

Jerry cleared his throat and said, "We don't know. There was nobody around when we got there. We got the call, and we were the only ones on the scene. I looked around after I saw this tourniquet, thinking someone had helped him. There was no way he could have put this on himself. The bullet must have hit his femoral artery and he was bleeding out fast. He must have lost consciousness in a matter of minutes, even seconds."

That didn't make sense, and I looked over at Bill Weathers.

He shrugged his shoulders and said, "My partner and I got there right after the EMS, and there was nobody else around. Like I said, somebody nearby heard the gunshot, and they saw somebody run out the entrance with a gun in his hand and wearing a ski mask. We've got a unit looking for him now. But there's only one way into that park—you've seen how high the fence is—and nobody else came out. It's not a big place, and there was nobody else in there. We went over every inch of it."

He then raised his eyebrows and shook his head. I looked over at Jerry again, and he did the same thing.

"How did this…Who put this on?" I asked. If what they were saying was true—and why wouldn't it be?—then how had this happened?

The room was silent, and we all looked down at Lenny Barker and his scarlet tourniquet.

Lenny survived the gunshot wound. He had lost a lot of blood but was not going to lose his leg. I visited him a couple of times while he was in the ICU and asked him what he remembered about the incident in Veteran's Park.

"I remember this guy coming up with a gun and asking for my money. When I told him I didn't have anything on me, I heard the gun go off and he took off running. That's it. Nothing else."

He didn't remember tying anything around his leg, and he didn't own a scarlet scarf.

My daughter and I drove in silence for a few moments, and then I looked over at her. She was staring straight ahead, her brow furrowed, and she was slowly tapping her chin with her index finger. Suddenly she stopped, and a smile began to warm her face. She turned to me and asked, "What do you think happened, Daddy? Who do you think tied that tourniquet?"

I turned back to the road and quietly asked, "Who do *you* think?"

She knew.

He heals the brokenhearted
and binds up their wounds.

Psalm 147:3

9

No Good Deed Goes
Unpunished (or So Some Say)

"Doggone it, I should have known better!"
Jay Stevens was just coming on duty and was walking up to the nurses' station, shaking his head and staring down at the floor.

"What's the problem?" I asked as I tossed the chart of room 2 into the discharge basket. Jay was a physician's assistant, working the overlap shift with me.

"On the way in tonight, I was driving down White Street," he began. "I came to a red light and this guy was standing there, looking at me. He held up his thumb, wanting a ride, and like a big dummy I opened the door."

"That's the first problem right there," Amy Connors said, shaking her head.

"Well, he seemed nice enough," Jay continued. "He was about my age and looked like he'd been working somewhere. He had on some coveralls that were covered with grease. I thought he might be a mechanic or something. Anyway, he thanked me and said he was going to Cherry Road, which was on my way."

"He didn't pull a gun on you?" Amy suddenly exclaimed, her eyes wide.

"No, nothing like that," Jay answered, calming her. "Like I said, he was nice enough, and we were just talking about stuff. I needed to get some gas, so I pulled into a station and got out and filled the tank. He stayed in the car until we got to Cherry Road. Then he got out and thanked me, and that's the last I saw of him."

"So what happened?" Amy asked, now sitting on the edge of her chair and leaning on the desk in front of her.

"Well, when I pulled into the parking lot, I reached over like I always do and took the CD out of the player to put it in my folder. I keep the folder on the floor out of sight, but it was gone! It holds all my CDs, at least eighty or ninety of them—they must be worth a couple of hundred dollars. But it was gone. He must have stuck it in his overalls while I was pumping gas."

"Are you sure it's gone?" I asked hopefully. "Maybe it's under the seat or something."

"No, I looked everywhere," Jay answered, shaking his head. "That guy stole it."

Amy leaned back in her chair and defiantly folded her arms across her chest.

"No good deed goes unpunished," she grumbled.

"What are you talking about?" Lori Davidson asked. She had just walked over from the medicine room. "You don't really believe that, do you, Amy?"

"Humph," the secretary muttered. "Of course I do. Seems that it happens just about every time you try to do somethin' nice for somebody. You remember me tellin' you about my neighbor's chickens, don't you?"

Lori shook her head, and Jay turned, leaning closer.

"No, what?" he asked.

"Well, you guys know we live out in the country," she began, unfolding her arms and putting her hands on the desk. "Well, one day my boy came runnin' into the house and hollerin' about some dog in the backyard. I followed him out there and sure enough, there was this mangy old mutt, some kind of collie-shepherd-beagle mix. He just stood there lookin' at us. Pitiful. He was all skin and bones and looked about ready to keel over. We had an old pen that we used to keep some goats in, and we put him in there. He didn't have any tag or anything, and he was a sweet dog, but he was just about dead. We fed him and nursed him back to health, and checked around to see if anyone was missing a dog. No luck there. The kids were gettin' attached to him, and I suppose I was too. Then one day, my boy went out to feed him and he got loose. Took off runnin' and headed straight through the woods to our neighbors. They kept some chickens and let 'em run loose during the day. That dog killed three of 'em before we could get there. Cost me fifty bucks."

She shook her head and slapped the desktop.

"Like I said, 'No good deed—'"

"What happened to the dog?" I asked.

"My husband found someone at work who wanted a huntin' dog and he took him. Says he's doin' great. Just has to keep him away from the chickens."

Jay chuckled and stood there, shaking his head.

"So, you gonna call the cops?" Amy asked him.

He thought for a moment, then said, "Yeah, I'd like to, but I don't have any idea who the guy is."

Lori looked over at him. "Maybe he needs them more than you. Just remember what Virginia Granger tells us. Always do the right thing."

She turned and walked back out to triage.

A few weeks later, I found myself once again standing at the nurses' station with Jay Stevens and Amy Connors. It was a Saturday evening, and the ER was humming. Lori Davidson was on her way back out to triage, when the ambulance doors suddenly opened and a young woman walked into the department. Lori looked over at her and stopped where she stood.

"Could we help you?" Amy asked the woman. She was standing in the hallway, looking around, eyes wide open.

"Yes," she said quietly, then stepped over to the counter beside me.

She was tall, slender, and dressed in worn slacks and an old sweat-suit jacket.

"I was here a week ago, with my child," she began to explain, still glancing nervously around the department.

Jay and I had stopped what we were doing and listened, waiting.

"I...my baby was sick, and after I saw the doctor, I left and went to the drugstore with her prescription. I didn't know how much it was going to cost, and I only had two dollars, but Amanda was really sick."

She stopped and looked at me and then down at Amy. Then she reached into her purse and took out a wrinkled twenty-dollar bill and put it on the counter.

"I want to return this," she said.

"Return it?" Amy asked.

"Yes," the woman replied. "When I got to the drugstore and looked in my purse, someone had put twenty dollars in there. I was able to get the medicine, and now I...I just want to bring this back and return it to whoever put it there. And I'd like to thank them if I could. I don't know what I would have done..."

Amy looked up at me, raised her eyebrows, and shook her head.

"I don't know who…" Amy began.

I turned around and looked at Lori. Our eyes met, and her face turned crimson. She quickly spun around and headed out to triage.

I looked at the young woman.

"We'll find out who that was, and let them know you came by," I told her. "And I'm sure she would want you to keep the money."

Amy looked up at the word *she*, then glanced down the hallway.

"But I—" she said quietly.

I picked up the rumpled bill and handed it to her.

"I'm *sure* she would want you to have this."

The young woman looked first at Jay, then Amy, and then me.

"Thank her for me," she whispered.

Then turning, she walked out of the ER.

Every time you do a good deed
you shine the light a little farther into the dark.
And the thing is,
when you're gone
that light is going to keep shining on,
pushing the shadows back.

Charles de Lint (1951–)

10

One Less Mystery

L ife presents us with some great mysteries, most of which will remain unsolved. However, thanks to one of our ER nurses, one of these significant conundrums has finally been solved. It involved a question long asked by those of us in the ER: *What do our patients talk about among themselves when there are no nurses or physicians around?*

It required no small sacrifice on the part of that nurse, Kathy Z. She had been out riding, when her horse bucked and she fell, breaking an ankle. She found herself lying on one of the stretchers in our four-bed minor trauma room, waiting on the orthopedist.

The curtains were drawn around her for privacy, and within a short time the other three beds had been filled with new patients. They had no idea she was a nurse, much less one of our staff members, and before long there was quite a conversation going on in the room.

There was a middle-aged woman on the stretcher next to Kathy, and she leaned over and pulled the nurse's curtain open.

"Oh my, honey," she said, looking down at her splinted ankle. "Looks like you done busted somethin' bad."

Kathy just nodded and reached out to close the curtain, but the movement sent shooting pain up her leg and she settled back on the stretcher.

"Well, I'm here with a headache," the woman said matter-of-factly. "Just going to get something for pain and then be on my way."

One of the ER doctors on duty walked into the room and over to the woman with the headache.

"Ms. Jones," he said as he stepped beside her.

The transformation was immediate and amazing.

"Oooooh!" Ms. Jones moaned loudly, clutching her temples and rocking back and forth on the bed. "My head is killing me!"

She kept moaning and rocking the whole time the doctor was in the room. When he finally left, she took a deep breath, sighed, glanced over at Kathy, and winked at her.

"You see, girl," she began to explain, "you've got to get their attention. And if that doctor doesn't order somethin' good, I'll just keep moanin' until he does."

Kathy had forgotten about the pain in her ankle and was trying to process what had just transpired, when the twenty-year-old man across the room suddenly began to moan and roll around on his stretcher. Kathy hadn't seen the ER doctor come back in, but this patient had.

"Oh, my belly," he groaned, his face contorted in pain and misery. "It's killin' me!"

The doctor walked over to the stretcher, pulled the curtains closed, and began to ask the young man about his pain.

Kathy heard bits and pieces of the conversation, but could only make out "weak and dizzy," "nauseated," and "almost passed out." These complaints were punctuated with "Ooh, it's killin' me!"

The ER doc left the room, and a few minutes later one of the technicians from the laboratory walked in. She approached the young man, made sure of his identity, and then said, "I'm here to draw some blood and get a urine specimen."

After a couple of minutes she walked out, carrying several vials of blood. She had handed him a container for his urine specimen and pointed to a bathroom across the hall.

"I'll be back for that in a few minutes," she had told him.

As soon as she left the room, he jumped up off the stretcher, looked straight at Kathy, and said, "Doggone it! It's Sunday night and all I wanted was a work excuse for tomorrow! They've been stickin' and pokin' me, and who knows what else they're gonna do! I'm outta here!"

And with that, he was out of the room and exiting the ER through the back entrance.

Kathy was still staring in amazement, when she was suddenly startled by a deep voice from behind the curtain in the corner of the room.

"Amateurs," the man said knowingly. "No experience. Just too impatient and dramatic. You've got to be calm and collected."

Kathy glanced over at Ms. Jones. The headache patient was staring in the direction of the voice and slowly nodding her head in agreement, waiting for his next words of wisdom.

"Yep," the man continued. "You just have to know what you're doin'. For instance, I'm here with back pain, and I expect to get somethin' good.

The first lesson is not to appear to know too much. Don't ever volunteer that your pain is a 10 on a scale of 1 to 10. That's a dead giveaway. Leave yourself some leeway, maybe a 7 or an 8. That way, it can always get worse and you might get something else for the pain. If you start at 10, you've got nowhere to go."

Kathy's jaw dropped. She had asked her patients this question for years, relying on their assessment of their level of pain and usually trusting their judgment. This was...well, this was astonishing. A dozen questions flashed through her mind and she was about to ask him one, when Ms. Jones spoke up.

"What if they don't ask you that?" she said to him. "I mean, about the 1-to-10 thing?"

"Oh, they will," the bodiless voice answered. "They always do."

Just then there were footsteps in the hallway and the ER doctor walked back into the room.

He stepped behind the curtain of the "voice" and began asking the man about his back pain.

"How bad is it?" the doctor queried.

"Oh, it's pretty bad," the patient answered quietly, in obvious pain but with a brave and controlled restraint.

"Can you rate that on a scale of 1 to 10?" the doctor asked.

"A what?" the man asked. "A scale?"

"Yes," the doctor answered. "With 1 being little pain, and 10 being the worst you've ever had."

"Oh, I see," the man said softly. "Let me think about that for a moment."

Kathy was looking at Ms. Jones. The headache lady was nodding and smiling. Then she looked over at Kathy and winked again.

"Well, Doctor," the voice spoke again. "If you ask it that way, I suppose I would have to say..."

Without mysteries,
life would be dull indeed.

CHARLES DE LINT (1951–)

11

ALWAYS A PONY

Ray Coggins had been a part of the hospital for as long as I could remember. Actually, for as long as anyone could remember. He had started as a teenager in the maintenance department of the old county hospital and had never left. Twenty years ago, he had moved into the new hospital with the rest of us, and now at age seventy-two, he enjoyed the distinction of being our oldest employee.

He might not use the word *enjoy,* since just last week the administration had served notice that he had long since passed the mandatory retirement age and would have to leave. Fifty-four years, and now asked to pack his bags. But just like all of the other troubles that had befallen this kind and caring man, this news had seemed to bother the rest of us more than it bothered him. Knowing Ray, though, that shouldn't have surprised any of us.

Ray had known the old hospital like the back of his hand, knew her peculiarities and weaknesses, and knew what she needed to keep limping along. He had made it a point to know the new one as well, and though repeatedly passed over for promotions, he was always the first one to respond to some plumbing or electrical disaster. And when Hurricane Hugo had blown through the upstate, he had been there hours on end, never going home, always helping out wherever he could.

But it hadn't stopped there. The whole town was reeling from the storm, and when he finally left the hospital and went back home, he found his neighborhood covered in fallen trees and limbs and without electricity. With no hesitation, he gassed up his chain saw and went from yard to yard, freeing up driveways and doorways. He only took a break when a wayward tree limb sprang back, causing his saw to rip a gash in his left thigh.

"Does it need stitches, Doc?" he had asked me.

The wound was gaping open and needed attention.

"It's just that Mrs. Jenkins across the street needs some help," he explained. "And I need to get back before dark."

A few years ago, Ray had sheepishly come into the ER and asked me to take a look at one of his toes. It wasn't hurting, and he didn't remember doing anything to it. Something just wasn't right. That *something* turned out to be undiagnosed and untreated diabetes, and the next day Ray had three toes on his right foot amputated. A year after that, he almost lost his left leg. It was only going to be a matter of time before this disease destroyed him.

Yet his spirit remained unchanged, and the warm smile that seemed to precede him into a room was always there. To us in the ER, how that was possible was always a mystery, a constant source of wonder, and one of the reasons everyone in the department loved him. We didn't see a lot of that with many of our patients. It seems that a tiny splinter can send some people into a fit of anger, even rage. And the smallest inconvenience can push a lot of us over the edge. Not so with Ray. He just accepted everything that came his way and made the best of it.

Early this morning, before the ER had really awakened, Ray had come strolling down the hallway on his way out to the ambulance entrance. The automatic doors had been hanging up and he was here to repair them.

As he passed me at the nurses' station, he stopped and said, "Well, good mornin', Doc. You doin' okay?"

I put down the chart I held and turned to face him.

"Ray, I've been looking for you," I told him.

"Whatcha break now?" he asked, his eyes laughing at me, and that same wide and warm smile on his face.

I glanced over to the empty triage hallway and quietly said, "Come over here a minute."

He followed me into the privacy of this small area and I again turned to face him.

"I just want you to know that we're going to miss you around here," I began, studying his face for some response. I knew he didn't want to leave the hospital. He had no immediate family, and this was all he had really known for the past five and more decades. *We* were his family.

"Well, you know…I guess it's time." His eyes were studying mine now, searching my heart, sensing the sadness I was feeling. But his smile never wavered.

"It's just that…well, Ray, what are you going to be doing with yourself? You've been doing this a long time, and—"

"Doc, don't worry about me," he interrupted, reaching out and laying a giant yet gentle hand on my shoulder. "I'll find plenty of stuff to do."

It was only a flicker, and then it was gone. But there in his eyes I could see the sadness, the loss he was experiencing. And I wanted to say or do something to help this man, this friend.

"You know I talked with the administrator," I said. "I told him you were—"

"I know you did, Doc," he interrupted again. "And I appreciate it. But sometimes…well, sometimes things just have to happen."

He was patting my shoulder now, and I was struggling for something else to say.

"Doc, I want to tell you something. Something my grandmother told me when I was just a chap. But I've never forgotten it, not to this very day."

He took his hand from my shoulder and leaned back against the wall behind him. He was rubbing his hands together now, studying them, and measuring his words.

"Grandma told me once about a young farmhand, probably only fifteen or sixteen years old. One day, the foreman came up to him and told him he needed a big pile of horse manure loaded into a cart. It was bad, smelly work, that's for sure. But that boy just dug in and started workin'. He was even smilin' while he did it. A couple of hours later, the foreman came back just as the boy was finishin' up. The kid was wipin' the sweat from his forehead, leanin' on his shovel, and just standin' there smilin'. Well, as you can imagine, that puzzled the foreman somethin' awful, and he just had to ask the boy how he could do that work and still be happy about it, still be smilin'. The boy just looked up at the foreman and said, "Well, sir, I thought that with all of this horse manure here, there just has to be a pony nearby."

I couldn't help but chuckle at Ray's story, and his eyes seemed to be twinkling more than ever. I thought for a moment, and began to understand what he was telling me.

"But Ray," I ventured carefully, "what if there's no pony here?"

He stood up straight now, and tucked his thumbs into the belt of his pants.

"Dr. Lesslie," he said gently, yet with a firm resolution that surprised me, "there's *always* a pony."

A pessimist sees the difficulty in every opportunity;
an optimist the opportunity in every difficulty.

Winston Churchill (1874–1965)

12

SOME SWEET REFRAIN

Doris Todd pulled into the parking lot of Meadowview Park, turned off her car, and just sat there. The single-storied retirement center sprawled in several directions among the tall oak trees. It was an older structure, certainly not threatening and maybe even inviting with its quaint Southern charm. Yet Doris was reluctant to get out of her car and go inside.

She had done so dozens of times before, but she had never felt this sense of dread, of foreboding. She knew it was going to be different today.

Doris had been a nurse practitioner for more than two decades, and for the past ten months had been one of the practitioners on the staff of Meadowview. She came out once a week to check on her patients, make sure their medications were in order, and examine them for any physical changes that needed to be addressed. All too frequently she would find their beds empty, or occupied by a new resident. Her patients, who had quickly become her friends, would have passed on.

That's why she still sat in her car. She was afraid Kate Weatherhead's bed was going to be empty. And Kate was more than just a friend.

Doris's mother and Kate had grown up together, along with Kate's younger sister, Sarah. When Kate had started developing signs of early Alzheimer's, it was Doris who Sarah had come to, seeking advice. That had been five years ago—five difficult years. And now it was clear that Kate was nearing the end of her struggle with this terrible disease. Last week, Doris had taken Sarah out into the hallway, intending to tell her, but Sarah had already known.

"I know, Doris—it's just a matter of time now, any time," she had quietly said. Then glancing back at the open door of Kate's room she added, "She's ready. I don't think she even knows if I'm in the room or not."

"I'm sure she does," Doris had responded, hoping that was the reality and wanting to offer some encouragement. "She can sense your presence, and she's comforted by that."

"I'd like to think so," Sarah answered, slowly shaking her head. "But I just don't know. The only time she seems to be with me at all is when I sing one of her favorite hymns to her, 'Amazing Grace.' It always brings a little smile to her face, I think. But maybe I'm imagining that. I just don't know."

And now, a week later, Doris was here again, wondering what she would find this afternoon. *Would it be over? Would Kate have found peace at last, and would her bed be empty?*

With a deep sigh, the nurse got out of her car and walked down the flagstone sidewalk leading to the covered entrance of Meadowview. She nodded her head at the receptionist and turned left down the hallway leading to Kate's room.

The door was partially open and Doris tapped lightly on it, waiting for a response but not expecting one.

After what seemed forever, there came a faint and whispered response. "Come in."

It was Sarah's voice, and Doris quietly pushed the door open and walked into the room. As usual, Sarah had pulled her chair up beside Kate's bed and was leaning in close to her sister, gently holding and rubbing her slender, worn hand.

Doris knew immediately that this was the last time she would see Kate alive. Her breathing was slow and erratic, and her color was pale, almost gray.

She stepped over behind Sarah and put a hand on her shoulder.

"Doris, she's…" Sarah faltered, the words too painful to utter.

"I know, Sarah," Doris said quietly, gently patting her shoulder. "I know."

It was just the three of them, three friends, and there was nothing else but this one moment, this one place.

"Doris," Sarah said, looking up at her, "would you sing to Kate with me? I know she won't hear us. She didn't respond at all a little while ago to 'Amazing Grace.'"

"Sure I will," Doris answered, struggling with the words as her voice nearly broke. This was a holy moment, and she was humbled and honored to be here with these two women. "What do you want to sing?"

Sarah looked over at her sister and then back to Doris. "For some reason, there's been a song running through my head all day. It was our father's favorite hymn and I remember singing it at his funeral. Do you know 'Blessed Assurance'?"

"Yes, I do," Doris responded, smiling. It had always been one of her favorites as well.

The words were barely out of her mouth, when Sarah began singing.

"Blessed assurance, Jesus is mine..."

They sang together quietly, the words having a special meaning to each of them. Doris sensed a growing peace, something she had needed, a lifting of the anxiety she had experienced out in the parking lot while sitting alone in her car.

She squeezed Sarah's shoulder in gratitude, and then suddenly both of them tensed. Together, each drew in a sharp breath. They struggled to continue singing as they stared down at Kate's near-lifeless face.

They had reached the refrain of the hymn, and as they watched, Kate's lips began to move and she silently mouthed the words along with them: "This is my story..." She didn't stop until they were finished, and then she just lay there, her breathing becoming more and more shallow.

An hour later, Kate Weatherhead was gone.

Not long after, Sarah and Doris walked out of the building, their arms around each other. They were still singing.

This is my story, this is my song,
Praising my Savior, all the day long.

Fanny J. Crosby (1820–1915)

13

Merry Christmas to *All*

Holidays in the ER are always busy, especially Christmas. And if you're unfortunate enough to have to work, you learn to brace yourself. Others are at home with friends and family, surrounded by love and filled with a tangible sense of peace and well-being. We in the ER, however, spend the day a little differently. We'll see a long parade of people with real and imagined problems, many apparently oblivious to the holiday. And as the day passes into evening, we'll start to see alcohol-related injuries: auto accidents, wounds from fistfights, knife fights, and gunshots. It can be a hard place to find and keep the Christmas spirit.

But not always.

Christmas Eve, 7:15 p.m. Shift change had just occurred, and most of the staff was gathered at the nurses' station, organizing ourselves for the next twelve hours.

The automatic ambulance doors swung open and one of our EMS units wheeled their stretcher into the department. It was occupied by an all-too-familiar sight.

"Joe, what in the world are you doing here tonight?" Lori Davidson asked, walking over to where the paramedics had temporarily stopped, waiting for a room assignment.

Joe Lyons was one of our "regulars." He was a chronic alcoholic and had probably spent more time in the ER than I had, usually visiting us at least once or twice a week.

A little over a month earlier, we had arranged for him to go to one of the local shelters, and according to the people who ran it, he was making an effort to be a team player. They had thought he might be able to stay there a while, but here he was again, back in the ER—and with one of his usual complaints.

"Nurse Lori, my heart is killin' me!" he moaned, clutching his chest.

Joe was seventy-three years old. He had already had two heart attacks and suffered the ravages of years of cigarettes and alcohol abuse. Every time he came to the ER we had to "work him up," giving him the benefit of the doubt and making sure nothing serious was going on.

Lori directed the paramedics to room 4, where they quickly deposited Mr. Lyons and headed back out into the cold night and more waiting business.

After I had examined him, I stood silently by his stretcher and stroked my chin. I was a little confused. He was stone-cold sober, a condition in which I had rarely if ever seen him. He was still complaining of chest pain, but his exam was normal.

We checked an EKG, a chest X-ray, and lab work, all of which were fine. Once we had all his studies, I went back to room 4 to talk with him.

"Joe, it looks like everything's okay," I explained to him. "There's no evidence of anything going on with your heart, and we'll be able to send you back to the shelter."

He looked down at his folded hands and didn't say anything.

I was standing at the nurses' station a few minutes later when Lori walked up.

"Dr. Lesslie," she said hesitantly. "It's Joe. He doesn't want to leave."

"What do you mean, 'He doesn't want to leave'?" I impatiently responded. "What's the problem?"

The ER was busy, with almost every bed full, and I just didn't have time for this.

"He doesn't want to go back to the shelter," Lori said quietly. "He wants to stay with us."

Lori was one of our best nurses—seasoned and experienced. She knew how busy we were and how much we needed the bed. There must be something else going on here.

"Lori…"

"Please, Doctor, do this as a favor for me," she pleaded. "Do you want to know what he told me? He said we were the only family he had, the only people left who really cared for him. He said the people at the shelter were nice, but not like us. It's different here. And he just wants to stay a little while longer."

"Lori…"

"Dr. Lesslie, it's Christmas Eve," she implored.

Then, with a twinkle in her eye she added, "And don't be a Scrooge."

I thought for a moment. She was right, of course—it *was* Christmas Eve. And so what if we tied up a bed for another hour or so?

Suddenly a thought occurred to me.

"Lori, isn't the hospital providing some kind of meal for the staff tonight? Aren't they going to bring around something for each department?"

She nodded her head and was about to say something when I interrupted her.

"Why don't you take Joe back to the lounge and make him comfortable? We can call the kitchen and arrange for an extra meal, and he can eat with us."

"That's a great idea," she said, starting to turn and reach for one of the phones. She stopped and looked over at me. "Maybe you're not such a Scrooge after all."

It was a little before midnight when I was able to break away for a few minutes and head back to the lounge. Joe sat at the lone table, surrounded by several nurses and secretaries. The king and his court.

I fixed a plate for myself and sat down across the table from him, and after a few minutes, we were alone.

"Doc, I know I'm a bum," he said, surprising me with his bluntness. "You and I both know I'm an alcoholic, a deadbeat. Not good for nothin' anymore. Haven't been for a long time. But I want you to know one thing."

He paused and I looked up into his pale, bloodshot eyes. There were tears in them, and a few on his cheeks. I wanted to look away, but couldn't.

"I'll never forget what you all done for me tonight. Never."

We heard the doorknob rattle and both of us looked over as Lori came into the room.

"Okay, Joe, it's time to call a cab," she told him, smiling and walking over to the table. "It's officially Christmas morning and time to head back to the shelter."

I studied his face and watched as a dark, troubled cloud passed over it. He looked down at his empty plate and his shoulders slumped.

"Yeah, you're right," he murmured.

He slowly stood up, shaking some bread crumbs from his lap.

"Just a minute, Lori," I said. "Isn't there an open bed in the observation unit?"

She looked over at me, confused. And then she understood.

"Yes, there is," she answered. "Just one left."

"Why don't we let Joe bed down there for the night?" I said. "It's mighty cold outside, and besides, it's pushin' one o'clock."

"That sounds fine to me," she answered, smiling. Then she took the man's hand and led him out into the hallway.

At seven a.m., our Christmas-morning relief walked begrudgingly up to the nurses' station. A few minutes later, I was talking with one of my partners when Joe shuffled out of the OBS unit and over to where we stood.

He struggled a little putting on his coat and then looked over to me.

"Thanks again, Doc," he said smiling. Glancing behind the counter he added, "And thanks, Nurse Lori. Merry Christmas to all of you."

Then he turned and walked out of the department.

My partner stared after him and said, "Joe Lyons?"

I was smiling, and then I nodded my head.

"Yes, that was Joe," I told him.

...and to all *a good night.*

14

Tempus Fugit

2:30 a.m. Frank Marshbanks and I were sitting at the nurses' station, drinking some old, barely warm coffee. He had just finished a case in the OR and had stopped by on his way home.

"You guys should be able to do better than this," he grumbled, holding up his cup for me to see.

"One step at a time," I answered.

We had only been in Rock Hill a little over six months and I was still learning my way around the hospital. Frank had been a surgeon in Rock Hill for more than thirty years, and we had quickly forged a solid friendship. I knew I could count on him for help with my patients, so I didn't hesitate to lean on him for advice.

Just then, one of our techs came shuffling down the hall. He was older, probably in his sixties, tall and slender. As he passed the nurses' station he looked over at Frank, tipped his head, gave a familiar wave of his hand, and said, "Time flies when you're having fun, Doc. Better get some sleep."

"Don't worry, Ernie," Frank called after him. "I will."

Ernie disappeared into the triage hallway as Frank turned to face me. He was slowly stroking his chin as he said, "You know, Ernie's right about that."

"About what?" I asked, not sure of his point. "About you needing some sleep?"

"No, about time flying," he answered. "But it flies whether you're having fun or not."

Frank put his half-empty cup on the counter, leaned back in his chair, and looked directly at me.

"You're spending a lot of time here in the ER, aren't you?" he stated more than asked.

He was right. I *had* been working a lot of hours lately, and more night shifts. That always messed up the schedule at home. But we were short two doctors and everyone had to help out.

"We've got a new doc coming in a couple of months," I answered. "And things should get better then."

The look on his face didn't change. Then his eyes squinted a little as he studied mine. His gaze was becoming uncomfortable, and I looked away.

He shifted in his chair, crossed his legs, and folded his hands behind his head. Then he cleared his throat and began.

"I don't know if you're aware of this, but I grew up in a small town. Three, maybe four thousand people. There were only two family docs and my father was one of them. They did everything back then—delivered babies, yanked out gallbladders, took care of heart attacks, and even pulled a few teeth. Can you imagine doing that today? Needless to say, he was busy. Worked all the time. And when he wasn't working he was either in church or trying to catch up on his sleep."

Frank paused, took a deep breath, and stared beyond me.

"My memories of my father when I was a child are of his lab coat hanging in the hall, smelling of ether. I can remember standing there by the stairs, all alone, hugging it and pressing the worn-out cotton against my face. And I can remember his heavy footsteps coming in the door late at night, when I was supposed to be asleep. He had a kind of shuffle. One of his feet dragged just a little, and it seemed the later at night it got, the worse it got. I'll never forget that."

He stopped and looked directly at me.

"How many kids do you and Barbara have?" he asked.

"Four," I said. "The youngest is a little over a year old."

"Four," he repeated softly. "There were four of us. Three girls and me."

He looked down at the floor for a moment, then continued.

"It seemed like I never saw my father. There were Sundays when he would sit next to me in our family pew at church, but more often than not he would be called away. Somebody was sick, or in labor, or…it didn't matter. He was gone. After high school I went to UNC, pre-med of course, and then to medical school. Looking back, I know it was the right thing for me to do, but there were times…there were times when I wondered if I was just doing it for him. He was excited about me becoming a doctor. We even talked about going into practice together. But you know, Robert, the older I got, the more I realized I didn't know the man. It took a broken hip to do that, to bring us together."

He uncrossed his legs, leaned forward in his chair, and began rubbing his hands together.

"It was in May of my second year in medical school. Dad fell going out the back door of his office and broke his hip. That was the only summer our class had off during those four years of med school, and I spent it at home helping him in the office. He could get around some and was determined to work, but he needed some help. For those three months, we spent every day together. I helped him examine patients, drove him around to house calls, and even helped him with his surgeries. We did a little of everything, and it was great. And I realized then that we liked each other."

I thought his voice had trembled a little as he said this, but there was only a slight pause and he went on.

"But there was something about that summer that bothered me, that made me angry. I couldn't help but think about the twenty-five years I had spent without him, without really knowing him...my father. And realizing what a great guy he was only made it worse. He had spent more time with Mamie Spencer and her nonexistent maladies than he had with me, his only son. And all the businessmen in town and the elders in our church had always liked and respected him and thought he was a good man. But he had never taken the time to get to know his own son. I resented that. I never told him, but I resented it.

"By the end of that summer, though, I had resolved those feelings. I counted those three months we spent together as a beginning, something that we would always have, and that we could build on. I felt great when I went back to school in September. We would call each other at least once a week, and for the first time we were really able to talk with each other."

Frank sighed and his voice became quiet.

"One night early that October, Mama called. Dad had had a stroke, and was dead. That was it. He was gone."

He paused again, and when he continued, his voice was unmistakably trembling. I studied his face, and my chest tightened as I listened to this sixty-year-old surgeon share these memories with me.

"You know, that still makes me mad as heck. There was nothing fair about that. Nothing at all. But Robert, I learned a lesson, one that I try to think about every day. All we have is this moment. Right now...today.

Sounds trite, but I've been there. I'm still there. And I didn't let my children grow up wondering who I am. My work is important to me, but my family has always come first. I'm not perfect, but that's the way I've tried to live."

He stood up, stretched, and put a heavy hand on my shoulder. And now he was smiling.

"My friend, your number-one job is your family. Make sure your kids know the good man you are, and make sure you know them."

He patted my shoulder a couple of times, then stepped away and turned toward the ambulance entrance. He stopped and faced me once again.

"Don't ever forget what Ernie said, Robert. Time *does* fly."

He stood there for a moment before turning once more and walking through the automatic doors. Then he disappeared into the night.

Time is the coin of your life.
It is the only coin you have,
and only you can determine how it will be spent.
Be careful lest you let other people spend it for you.

CARL SANDBURG (1878–1967)

15

To Disentangle Peace from Pain

I just don't know what else to do," Kathy Meyers said to me, a cup of now-cold coffee in her hand.

She was one of the best nurses in the department, and it was unusual to see her so frustrated. It was sleeting outside. The ER had been empty for the past hour, and we had been sitting in the lounge talking. Our conversation had turned to our families.

We had known each other for several years, and we shared a trust that allowed us to be completely open. I had known about the rift between Kathy and her sister, Alexis, but tonight I realized how deep and painful that estrangement had become.

Both sisters were in their early thirties, and something had happened between them three or four years earlier—something that had drastically changed their relationship. I had asked Kathy what that had been, what event or circumstance could possibly have caused such a devastating effect, but she couldn't remember.

"I'm really not sure," she had told me, shaking her head. "We had argued about something, some trivial matter, and things just blew up. We had always been close, but things were said, and…and then we just didn't talk. She only lives an hour-and-a-half from here, but I haven't seen her in more than three years."

There were tears in her eyes, as there always were when we talked about this. Early on, there had been a palpable anger and an impregnable wall of defense. But now there was only this frustration, this need to make things right again but not knowing how to do it.

This past Christmas, Kathy had invited the whole family to a church service on Christmas Eve and then for dessert at her home. Reluctantly Alexis had agreed, and there had seemed to be a workable though tense truce. But something had happened in the kitchen, something was said and misinterpreted, and Alexis huffed out. That ended any small progress that had been made in repairing their relationship.

Then a few months ago, their mother had been sick. When Kathy had visited, the subject of Alexis had come up. This was obviously on her mother's heart, and it grieved both of her parents greatly.

"What did your mother have to say?" I had asked her.

"She told me that she and Dad were praying for the two of us, and for our healing this. And that I needed to be praying too. And…that we needed to forgive each other."

"And?" I asked her.

"I *do* pray about this, Dr. Lesslie," she stammered, looking away from me. "But it's so hard, and I don't know what I did to deserve her treating me like this, and if only she would…"

She stopped and looked down at the floor, her tears falling into her lap.

"It's just so twisted," she whispered painfully. "So tangled."

She sighed heavily and her shoulders slumped.

After a few moments she looked up at me.

"Maybe it's not Alexis I need to be praying for," she said quietly. "Maybe it's *me*. I need to find a way to forgive her. And I need to find a way to be forgiven."

I sat there with her, silent, not needing to say anything. Kathy knew what she needed to do.

A few weeks later, we had another chance to talk. Kathy's whole demeanor had changed and she was bursting to share something with me.

She pulled me aside into the medicine room, out of the chaos of the ER, and said, "I called Alexis last night. And it's…it's…"

She was struggling for words, her emotions overpowering her.

"What did you say to her?" I finally asked, trying to help.

"I said, 'Alexis, please forgive me.' That's all I knew to say, and I just stood there, holding the phone and praying."

There were tears again on her cheeks, but these were tears of joy. She was smiling at me.

"And after what seemed like forever, she said the only thing she needed to say. She said 'Kathy, I love you.'"

...To disentangle peace from pain,
And make your broken people whole.

FROM THE HYMN "WE CANNOT MEASURE HOW YOU HEAL"

BY JOHN BELL AND GRAHAM MAULE

16

THE CHOICES WE MAKE

Amy Connors slid the lab slip across the countertop to me. There, at the bottom of the report, was what I wanted to see.

"Good," I said quietly, then attached the paper to the chart of the young man in room 1.

"Good that he's got mono?" Amy asked, looking up at me from her chair behind the nurses' station.

"Good that it's nothing worse," I told her, picking up the chart and heading over to the exam room where Kevin Mazingo and his mother were waiting.

The eighteen-year-old had come in with complaints of three weeks of fatigue, cough, aches and pains, a little bit of a sore throat, and some weight loss. His mother was concerned that he looked a little pale. And he did. He was anemic.

He also had swollen lymph nodes in his neck, and I could feel the tip of his spleen when he took deep breaths. He had a straightforward presentation for mononucleosis. But so had a twenty-year-old college student I had seen a month earlier. He had turned out to have lymphoma, and so I was a little gun-shy.

Kevin was sitting on the stretcher in room 1 with his long legs dangling over the edge. He was six-four, weighed a little over two-hundred-forty pounds, and even though sick, looked every bit the high-school football star he had become. He and his mother looked over at me as I entered.

"Well, we've got our answer."

I told them about the lab report and as I began to explain the best ways to deal with this infection, Kevin's shoulders slumped and he hung his head.

His mother looked over and put her arm around him.

"He's disappointed," she explained. "About the three to four weeks of rest."

Kevin looked up at me and said, "Dr. Lesslie, I've already missed a week of football practice, and our first game is in two weeks. Is there any way I'd be able to play?"

I knew this was a big deal for him. He was a local hero, and the area papers were full of stories of the college teams recruiting "the best high-school linebacker in the Southeast." He had narrowed his choices to Georgia, Tennessee, and South Carolina, and recruiters from those schools and more would be at his first game. But his father had been a star at Georgia and so had his coach, Donnie Kimball. There was little doubt that he would soon be a Georgia Bulldog.

But right now he needed to take care of himself. The mono had knocked him down, and he needed to rest.

I told him that again, and stressed to his mother the importance of avoiding physical contact. His spleen was enlarged and fragile, which was all part of the infection. They needed to be sure it had returned to normal size before he returned to football, and their family doctor could guide them with that.

She nodded and looked down at her son.

"I understand, Doctor, and we'll be sure he takes it easy."

Then she leaned close to her son and said, "Four weeks. Did you hear that? Four weeks. There's a lot at stake here, Kevin, and it's more than football. We just don't have a choice."

He hung his head again and slowly nodded.

Two weeks later on a Saturday night, I walked through the ambulance entrance. It was my last of three night shifts, and I was relieving Jason Woods, one of my partners. He was standing at the nurses' station, writing on a chart.

"Anything I can do to get you out of here?" I asked, stopping beside him.

He looked up, took a deep breath, and slowly blew it out.

"No, just writing up this last patient and then I'm done," he told me. "But what a day this has been! Especially the last couple of hours."

I glanced quickly around the department. It was calm for seven p.m., and Jason seemed to have things in order.

"I know, it *looks* okay," he said. "But we just finished up a traumatic arrest, and it was…" he hesitated, and Lori Davidson, standing behind us, spoke up.

"It was terrible. I don't know if I've ever been involved with anything so…devastating."

The door to major trauma was open. The light was off and the room empty.

"What happened?" I asked, turning to Jason.

He tossed the chart into the discharge basket, then stood there for a moment.

"You know the high-school kid," he began. "The football star over at Central, Kevin Mazingo?"

Suddenly my heart was in my throat and I couldn't answer him.

"Really awful," Jason went on. Then he looked over at me and said, "In fact, you made the diagnosis of mono a couple of weeks ago when he came in here."

"Yeah," I stammered, waiting.

"Well, he played last night and apparently had a great game. Went home and everything seemed to be fine, until this morning. He told his mother he didn't feel well and stayed in bed. She went in to check on him and couldn't wake him up. That's when she called EMS and everything got crazy. He was in shock and barely breathing. They got two lines going and when they arrived here, he had a pulse and a blood pressure of 60. But his hemoglobin was 4."

"4!" I exclaimed.

"Yeah, he had just about bled out," Jason responded. "Ruptured spleen, and his belly was full of blood. We got him to the OR as fast as we could, and they worked on him for more than three hours. But they couldn't save him. Eighteen years old and strong as an ox."

Jason stopped and looked over at Lori Davidson.

"And thanks for your help back in the family room, Lori," he told her. "I didn't expect all of that."

"What happened?" I asked, looking first at Jason and then Lori.

"Right before they took him around to the OR, Dr. Woods and I went back to the family room," Lori began, her voice subdued. "There were people everywhere. Kevin's parents were there, and his coach, Donnie Kimball. And there were other family members. Dr. Woods explained what was going on and that Kevin's spleen had been ruptured. That's when his mother exploded and started pounding Mr. Mazingo on his chest. Someone had to pull her away and get her calmed down. He just stood there and took it, and kept staring at the floor."

Jason interrupted. "From what I gathered, she had tried to keep Kevin from playing last night. But his father and Coach Kimball insisted it would be okay, and that he was fine. They apparently kept stressing that several college scouts would be there, and how important it was. I think they pressured him into playing."

"Or pressured *her* into letting him play," Lori added.

"There was a lot of guilt in that room," Jason said. "And a lot of blame. I can't imagine how they're going to deal with all this."

He walked around the counter, and I just stood there, drained and empty. This was such a tragedy, such a waste.

I remembered the last thing his mother had said.

"There's a lot at stake here, Kevin, and it's more than football. We just don't have a choice."

*Some choices we live not only once
but a thousand times over,
remembering them for the rest of our lives.*

RICHARD BACH (1936–)

17

Freddy, Say It Ain't So

Friday night, 11:45. EMS 2 had just responded to a call at 100 Pine Street. "Self-inflicted gunshot wound—right foot," the dispatcher had reported.

A crowd had gathered around the front porch when the paramedics arrived. They quickly retrieved the stretcher from the back of the ambulance, grabbed their equipment, and bounded up the rickety steps of the clapboard house. Their patient was sitting on the porch and leaning against the front door.

"Quick! Get me to the hospital! I'm bleedin' to death!"

The thirty-two-year-old man was rocking from side to side, holding a bloody towel around his right foot. His slurred speech and the stench of cheap wine suggested he might be less than sober. In fact, he was dead drunk.

"Let's take a look at this," one of the paramedics said, stooping down and starting to unwrap the injured limb.

"No! Don't do that!" the man hollered. "It'll start bleedin' again! Just get me to the hospital!"

His vital signs were stable, and it would be only a five-minute trip to the ER. The paramedics looked at each other and made up their minds.

"Okay," one of them told the man. "Let's get you on the stretcher."

As if by magic, their patient jumped unsteadily to his feet, wobbled down the steps, and plunked himself down on the gurney.

"Let's go!" he called to the startled medics. "What are you waitin' for?"

At the ER, the triage nurse directed them to minor trauma, where the paramedics deposited their patient, Freddy Lane, on one of the stretchers.

"Good luck, Doc," one of them said to me as I passed them in the hallway.

It wouldn't be the first time I had taken care of Freddy. That had taken place a couple of years earlier on a hot summer's afternoon.

"Rock Hill, this is EMS 2. We're on the way in with an allergic reaction. Multiple bee stings."

I recognized the voice of Denton Roberts, one of our paramedics. This could be bad, but he didn't sound very upset.

"Room 3 on arrival, EMS 2," Lori Davidson told him.

"Roger, room 3," Denton responded. "And Rock Hill, he's in no distress."

A few minutes later, the ambulance entrance doors opened, and our bee-sting patient was rolled into room 3.

"Vital signs are fine, Doc," Denton told me, shaking his head. "Not sure why, though. He's been stung more than a hundred times, but there's no wheezing or anything like that. Just some welts around the sting sites."

"What did he get stung by?" Lori asked, helping our patient get comfortable on the stretcher. He wore only a pair of old sneakers and some cut-off blue jeans. Red, angry welts covered most of his body. Nonetheless, his eyes were closed and there was a broad smile on his face. He certainly didn't appear to be in any distress.

"Honeybees," Denton answered. "Two hives, I think."

Lori and I must have been thinking the same thing. Together we asked, "Did you guys get stung?"

"No, we weren't anywhere near the bees," Denton said, chuckling. "We had to pull Freddy here out of a pond. He had run about a hundred yards after the bees got after him and jumped in the water to get away from 'em. Must have worked, 'cause there weren't any around when we got there."

"How did he get stung by so many bees?" Lori asked.

Denton looked down at the dozing, smiling Freddy and chuckled again.

"Freddy told us he saw the beehives and decided he wanted some honey," Denton began to explain. "Apparently he doesn't know much about beekeeping, although the two empty quarts of strawberry wine *might* have had something to do with his poor judgment. He just walked right up to the hives, opened them up, and took out a couple of frames. That got 'em goin', to say the least. And they got Freddy goin', right to the pond. He's probably too drunk to feel any pain."

"Mm-mmm," our patient murmured, grinning and licking his lips. And so we had met Freddy Lane.

I walked into the room and over to Freddy's bed. After I introduced myself, I moved to his right foot and began to carefully unwrap the bloody towel.

"Be careful, Doc!" he hollered, trying to grab my hand. "It's killin' me!"

"Hold steady, Mr. Lane," I told him. "I've got to take a look at this foot."

He was sitting up now and breathing in my face. The smell of alcohol was strong and offensive.

"Tell me, what happened here?" I asked him, removing the last of the towel. On the top of his foot was a small hole, with just a little blood trickling down from one side. His pulses were good, and there was very little swelling.

"Well, Doc," he began, more relaxed now that he could see his foot and be reassured he probably wasn't going to bleed to death, "it's like this. I was sittin' in the livin' room, watchin' TV. You know, just relaxin'—oww! Take it easy, boy!"

There was some stippling around the wound, and I was checking to see if it would easily wash off. I wasn't applying much pressure and was surprised by his sudden reaction.

Then just as suddenly, he relaxed and resumed his story.

"Yeah, like I was sayin'. I was sittin' in the livin' room, cleanin' my .32 Smith and Wesson, when all of a sudden...*bam!*"

I sat back in disbelief and stared at this man. He could barely sit up, he was so inebriated, and here he was telling me he had been cleaning a handgun.

"Well, that thing couldn'ta been loaded but doggone if it didn't go off. *Bam!* Scared me to death, and then I saw the hole in my foot and I knew I was gonna die. Right then and there."

He sat up, breathed heavily in my face again, and muttered, "How does it look?"

"We'll need to check it out," I told him, backing away as far and as quickly as I could.

We made a couple of X-rays, all of which were normal. Freddy had somehow managed to miss all of his bones and hadn't hit any major blood vessels or nerves. The wound would need to be carefully cleaned, and he would need a tetanus booster and antibiotics. He was going to live after all.

When I shared this good news with him he struggled awkwardly to his feet and began yelling at me.

"If you're talkin' about stickin' me with needles, you can forget it! I ain't havin' no part of that, so you might as well just send me home. Call a cab or get that ambulance back here. I'm ready to go! You ain't gonna poke around on my foot anymore! Just put a Band-Aid on it and I'll be on my way."

I tried to talk him into staying, explaining the potential for a serious infection and maybe even losing that foot. But he would have none of it. He was ready to go, and we couldn't keep him against his will. He refused crutches or even the offer of a wheelchair to get him out to the waiting room.

By this time he had sobered enough to half wobble, half hop down the hallway and out into the night. I stood at the nurses' station and just shook my head as the ambulance entrance doors closed behind him.

3:45 a.m. I was walking out of room 2 when I heard the EMS radio crackle. It was the dispatcher again, and she was notifying EMS of another emergency.

"Medic 2, respond code 3 to 100 Pine Street. Self-inflicted gunshot wound…of the left foot."

I stopped where I was and stared at the radio.
Freddy.

I wasn't born a fool.
It took work to get this way.
Danny Kaye (1913–1987)

18

An Unsung Hero

I wouldn't have known Danella had died if James Brewster had not almost died himself.

James had come into the ER late on a mid-winter night. He was complaining of chest pain and barely had a blood pressure. His EKG was classic for a massive heart attack. Thankfully he responded to a clot-buster. His EKG returned to normal, as did his blood pressure. We all breathed a sigh of relief.

I was sitting on a stool beside his stretcher, writing up his chart and not willing to leave his side. He was much better but still tenuous, and I didn't want to lose this affable eighty-year-old gentleman.

"Dr. Lesslie, where did you go to school?" he asked me, reclining easily on the stretcher with his hands folded across his chest.

I stopped writing and looked over at him.

"I did my undergraduate work at Erskine College," I answered. "And then went to medical school in Charleston."

"Erskine College," he repeated slowly, stroking his stubbled chin. "Due West, right?"

"That's right," I replied. "The big city of Due West. Just down the road from Antreville."

"I know all about Due West," he went on. "Had a lot of friends over there back in the day."

I put his chart on the counter behind me and leaned forward, resting my elbows on my knees. We had moved to Due West the summer before my freshman year in high school. My father had left his job just outside Charlotte to teach organic chemistry at Erskine. It was always good to cross paths with people who knew the area and the school.

"Did you ever live there?" I asked him.

"Oh no," he answered, chuckling. "Too small for me. Greenville was the closest I ever came. But I visited a lot. Had a good friend there…

actually my *best* friend. He was a preacher at the AME church just outside town. Elijah Valentine."

"Reverend Valentine?" I responded, recognizing the name.

"That's right, Reverend Valentine. He and I went to seminary together, and then he moved to Due West. Must have been there more than fifty, sixty years before he passed on."

I had heard Elijah Valentine had died when I was in medical school. He had always been active in the community—a kind and gentle man.

"I went to high school with his daughter, Danella," I told him.

James took a deep breath, sighed, and began rubbing his hands together.

"Now that was one special woman," he said quietly.

"Was?" I asked. *Could she be dead?* She and I were the same age.

"Yes, she's gone now," he answered, looking over at me. "I guess you haven't heard?"

I shook my head in response and looked at him. An uncomfortable empty feeling was spreading inside me. My life had moved on, and I had lost contact with most of my friends in high school and with the people I had grown up with.

"She died a few months ago," he continued. "I'm just glad Elijah passed before her, 'cause he wouldn't have wanted to see his daughter suffer the way she did. Cancer, they told her. Didn't know where it had come from, but when they found it, it was too late. She had a tough couple of months toward the end."

We sat silently for a moment.

"But that was one brave woman," he said, with admiration in his voice. "One brave woman."

I waited, hoping he would explain.

"She fought that cancer hard," he went on. "And she never gave up. She was always positive and cheerful. Almost happy. Now her daddy *would* have liked to see that. He would have been so proud of her. But he was always proud of her."

He cleared his throat and with a corner of his hospital gown wiped his eyes.

"I heard her speak at her church a few weeks before she died," he told me. "I've preached for a lot of years, but never shared the Word the way she did that day. She was anointed, touched by the Lord. And everybody in the room knew it."

He paused again, and then said, "Yes sir, she was one brave woman. Courageous, that's the word. Courageous."

That *was* the word for the Danella Valentine I had known. And I shared my own story with James Brewster.

We had just moved to Due West and I was a self-absorbed teenager, oblivious to most important things happening around me. It was August, sweltering, and school was to start in two weeks.

It would be my first year in high school. Dixie High School. Now *that's* a good Southern name. Before that year it had been an all-white school, but it was 1965 and things were changing—in Due West and all over the South.

One morning my father pulled me aside and said, "Robert, there are going to be some changes at Dixie when you start school. Two black students will be attending, a boy and a girl. I want you to treat them with respect."

That's all he said. He left me to sort it out on my own.

At first it didn't seem like such a big deal. There were more important things to consider, such as girls and basketball and...girls. But the nightly newscasts began showing films of confrontations and riots, and I began to understand the importance of what was happening. And I began to wonder who these two young people were, and why they would be willing to put themselves in such a difficult place.

When I met Danella Ruth Valentine, I began to understand. She was an interesting person, to be sure. Self-assured, engaging, and with a subtle edge of quiet defiance, she was able to handle the glares and occasional catcalls tossed her way as she walked the hallways of Dixie High School. Looking back, I'm not sure how she did it. I'm not sure that any of us understood how difficult a process this was for her and her family. Most of us were more concerned with how all of these changes would affect our own lives.

But Danella endured. We all did. There was never any violence at

Dixie, or really any tense or ugly moments, and we all somehow made it through those weeks and months and years. I didn't realize it at the time, but it was largely due to Danella's personality and character. And I came to understand that the choice of placing her at Dixie hadn't happened by chance. It turned out that a lot of thought and prayer had gone into the process. And there had been input from a lot of people in the community. My father was one of those people, along with Elijah Valentine. They had met regularly together and become friends. It had been a difficult decision for Elijah, sending his daughter out like that. But in the end, it was something he knew needed to happen, and that his daughter was the person to do it. She had never hesitated.

I finished talking and looked over again at James Brewster. There was a smile on his face and he was nodding at me.

"Courageous," he whispered.

Courage is contagious.
When a brave man takes a stand,
the spines of others are stiffened.

BILLY GRAHAM (1918–)

19

REDEEMED

H ey Doc, do you remember me?"
    I was standing in the hardware section of Lowe's, trying to find bolts for a gardening project. I hadn't noticed the middle-aged man who had walked up and was standing beside me.

That question always makes me a little nervous. Where had I seen this man? What did *he* remember about *me*? What important thing had I forgotten? Or maybe, should I run?

I turned and faced him, looked directly into his pale gray eyes, and tried to place him.

He was dressed appropriately for a Saturday morning—running shoes, khaki pants, and a blue sweat jacket. He had a list in his hand, the same as me.

"Al Carter," he said, smiling. Then he held out his hand and I took it. His grip was strong and he held my hand warmly, pumping it up and down enthusiastically.

Maybe I didn't need to run.

"You saw me in the ER a couple of times, probably ten or twelve years ago."

He let go of my hand but his eyes remained locked on mine.

"Al Carter…" I repeated slowly, still not remembering this man.

"I know, I know," he chuckled, breaking off his stare and stepping back a little. "You've seen a lot of people in the ER, and I was just one of them. I'm sure it's hard to remember every person. Heck, I'm sure it's *impossible*. Here, maybe this will help."

He reached down and grabbed the left sleeve of his jacket, then pulled it up to his elbow.

"Recognize your handiwork?" he asked, still smiling.

He raised his arm and rolled his wrist over, allowing me to see the front of it. Just at the base of his hand was a long scar—three inches at least—and long ago healed.

"Looks pretty good, doesn't it?" he said, glancing down and turning it from side to side.

I reached out and held his forearm, then fingered the smooth edges of the scar. It *did* look pretty good.

"Make a fist for me," I said, the ER doc in me taking over.

He flexed and extended his fingers several times and said, "See? Everything's working."

"Great."

There was a glimmer of a memory, still buried deep somewhere, and I still struggled to—

"You remember how this happened?" he asked patiently. "You remember why I did it?"

And there it was. Al Carter. I remembered everything.

"We need some help back in minor," Lori Davidson told me, wiping at the front of her uniform with a damp cloth. Blood had spattered—no, *sprayed*—across one entire side of it. "It's a lacerated wrist, self-inflicted, and looks like he might have gotten an artery."

"Give me a second," I told her. "I need to finish up with this child in 1."

A few minutes later I was headed down the hallway to minor. A police officer, standing in the doorway, looked over at me and nodded.

There was another officer in the room, standing beside the back-right stretcher, where our "bleeder" was lying. The man's left wrist was wrapped with a thick, blood-soaked bandage. He didn't look at me as I walked over, but kept staring straight ahead.

"Hey, Doc," Sergeant Jimmy Phillips called out. "Sorry about this one," he added, tilting his head toward the patient. "Don't know what he cut himself with, but it must have been sharp. Maybe the edge of his bunk or something,"

I stepped over to the side of the stretcher and reached out for the man's injured arm.

"Al Carter's his name," Phillips stated. "Just got busted a couple of days ago for parole violation. Guess he didn't want to go back to Columbia. He's lookin' at eight to ten, at least. And that's with good behavior, which isn't very likely."

Carter snarled up at the officer and then turned to me.

"How about some glue, Doc, or staples? I don't care what it looks like."

"Let the doctor do his job," the sergeant told him, stepping closer to the bed.

Carter didn't move while I carefully unwrapped the bandage. Lori had come back into the room and was getting a suture tray ready.

"Don't let it squirt on you like it did me," she warned. "It's pretty bad."

The last layer of the bandage came off and I barely missed being sprayed.

"Hold some pressure up here, Lori," I told her, pointing to an area just above the gaping laceration.

He had meant business. There was only one laceration, long and deep, with no signs of hesitation marks, no evidence of second thoughts. He knew what he had wanted to do and he had done it.

I pulled up a stool, sat down, and got to work.

"You've probably seen Al here before, Doc," Phillips said, leaning back against the countertop and examining his fingernails. "He's had several… accidents."

"Yeah, *accidents*," Carter repeated, cutting his eyes toward the officer.

I did remember seeing this man a few months earlier. He had come in after wrecking his motorcycle out on Highway 21. He'd been lucky—there were just some bad areas of road rash, but nothing broken.

Then I remembered something else. He had been involved in an auto accident at an exit off I-77. Police officers had brought him in that night as well. He'd been drinking, hit a guardrail, and rolled his vehicle. Somehow he had escaped with only a few scratches. The woman with him had been dead at the scene.

That's what had sent him to Columbia the first time. He had been convicted of involuntary manslaughter and sent to prison. That would be difficult to get over, and I wondered if that was what had changed him into the hard man lying in front of me. Or had he always been hardened?

He stared straight ahead the entire time I was suturing and didn't say a word. And he hadn't flinched when I injected the lidocaine. He was a tough guy, and I was glad his right wrist was handcuffed to the other side of the stretcher.

It took almost an hour to put him back together, but the result looked pretty good.

"There," I said, taking off my gloves and tossing them on the tray. "That should do it."

He glanced down at his wrist and muttered, "Good job, Doc. But some glue would have done fine."

"Carter…" Phillips grumbled.

I raised my hand and shook my head.

"It's fine, Jimmy. We just need to be sure he's not back here in a couple of hours with the other wrist cut open."

"Don't worry about that," the sergeant said, his voice low and threatening. "If he does this again, it'll be in Columbia, and not in Rock Hill. You can be sure of that."

Carter was sneering at the officer as I left the room.

"Bulky dressing?" Lori asked, taking some bandaging supplies out of the cabinet.

"Sure, that's fine." And then I walked up the hallway.

That was the last time I had seen Al Carter or heard anything about him. And now he was standing in front of me in Lowe's, in the hardware department. I must have backed up a little because he raised his hands and said, "Doc, I'm a different man now. Not the same jerk you sewed up in the ER."

I was embarrassed by my reaction—I hadn't meant to offend this man. Yet, he was Al Carter, and…

"You know what, Dr. Lesslie," he said, his voice quiet. "There are two women who are responsible for changing my ways, for showing me the path."

One must be his mother, and I was sure I had never met her. And the other? Maybe his grandmother.

"They both worked in your ER," he continued, his gray eyes fixed on mine.

"In the ER?" I repeated, taken by surprise.

"Yeah. It was one of your nurses." He went on to describe Lori Davidson. "While she was bandaging my wrist, she whispered to me that there was nothing I had ever done that wouldn't be forgiven, once I knew Jesus.

And she said something else I never forgot. She said he already knew me—that he had *always* known me."

He paused and I watched him closely. The only emotion in his voice or on his face was that of peace, and a contagious joy. He was happy to be telling me this.

"And the other woman was that bulldog of a head nurse of yours. She got right in my face and said, 'Son, get your life straight. It's the only one you've got.'"

He shook his head and laughed.

"My prison time wasn't easy, but I remembered what those two said, and I changed. I really changed, Doc. I'm married now, with a kid on the way."

He stopped suddenly and looked around.

"Oh, that reminds me! I'm supposed to be getting some paint for the nursery! Great to see you again, Dr. Lesslie."

He turned and hurried down the aisle, leaving me alone with my thoughts and the list in my hand.

Then he suddenly stopped, spun around, and raised his left arm in the air. Smiling and pointing to his wrist he called out, "And thanks again!"

It is not the healthy who need a doctor,
but the sick.
I have not come to call the righteous,
but sinners.

Jesus, in Mark 2:17

20

Not So Tuff

We are taught self-reliance from the time we begin to crawl. Maybe even before that. So it should come as no surprise that for most of us, this sense of self-reliance becomes an idol, something we can use to replace the Lord in our lives. We grow to depend more on ourselves and less on him. That's really the opposite of the way things are intended to be. We should be growing stronger in our sense of weakness, and growing to be more at peace with our utter dependence. Sometimes we need to be reminded.

Our older son, Robbie, had been scheduled for some nonemergent abdominal surgery. He was around nine years old at the time. His surgeon, a close friend of ours, had once again described the procedure.

"I don't expect anything unusual," Jason had reassured us. "And this should only take about forty-five minutes."

Understandably, Barbara was nervous, and she spent most of that time pacing the room. I knew the surgery wasn't life-threatening, and besides, I was an ER doc. I was used to handling all manner of emergencies and catastrophes, and did so with calmness and confidence. That's what we were supposed to do. "Don't ever let 'em see you sweat."

When the surgeon tapped on the door, stepped into the office, and smiled at us, we knew things had gone well and everything was okay.

"Robbie's fine," he told us. "He's around in recovery and should be heading up to his room in about an hour. You can go up there whenever you want."

Barbara thanked Jason and gave him a hug.

I stepped over to the door and said, "I'm going around to recovery and check on him."

My hand was resting on the doorknob, when Jason called out to me.

"Robert, you might want to wait a while. I'm not sure you want to see him right now."

Not see him right now? What was he trying to say?

I hesitated, but only for a moment. Again, I was an ER doc and had stood knee-deep in blood and guts, had cracked open chests and massaged dying hearts, and had put barely recognizable faces back together.

"I'll be back in just a minute," I told him, and headed out of the office and around the corner.

A sign at the entrance read, "Do Not Enter." I pushed the door open and stepped into the large room.

There were six stretchers in the unit, but only one was occupied. Debbie Whitesides, a friend of mine, was the nurse on duty. She was standing beside my son's stretcher, blocking my view of him as I walked over toward them.

"Hey, Debbie," I called out to her.

She turned around, surprise in her eyes and voice as she said, "Dr. Lesslie, what are you—"

I had reached the foot of the stretcher and looked down at my son. He was lying on his back, his arms by his side and a sheet drawn up to the middle of his bare chest. His eyes were closed and his facial muscles were relaxed. He was unconscious and looked like he was...

"It's okay, Debbie," I started to say. "I..."

The room started to spin and then began to grow dark. My knees were buckling—I had no control over my body. I was headed to the floor, and there was nothing I could do about it.

Suddenly there were two strong arms around me, and I was being gently lowered to a sitting position. It was Jason. He had followed me into recovery, knowing what I was going to find.

"It's okay, Robert," he said quietly. "I've been on the floor too. It's different when it's one of yours—especially your child. You know, you don't always have to be strong."

Such is the destiny of all who forget God...
What they trust in is fragile.

Job 8:13-15

21

Hidden Treasure

"You know, Robert, the writers of the Old Testament must have had a good sense of humor."

The statement took me by surprise, and I rolled back on the stool I was sitting on. I adjusted my glasses with the back of my gloved hand, and I looked up at the elderly woman on the stretcher in front of me. She had caught her left forearm on a screen-door handle, which had ripped a large gash in her paper-thin skin. I was doing my best to clean the wound and glue the edges back together. It was going to take a while.

"Sarah, what exactly do you mean by that?"

The eighty-year-old woman had my attention, and I knew this should be interesting. I had known her since we moved to Rock Hill more than twenty-five years ago and had always appreciated her sharp wit and keen perception. Nothing about that had changed. I waited for her response.

Just then one of our nurses, Lori Davidson, walked into the room to ask if I needed anything.

"Young lady, would you please reach into my pocketbook and hand me my Bible?" Sarah spoke up, pointing to the purse on the floor beside her.

Lori reached down, retrieved the surprisingly thin black leather-bound book, and handed it to her. With unexpected dexterity, Sarah used her right hand to hold her Bible, thumb to somewhere near the middle, and then turn a few pages.

"There, that's it," she said with satisfaction. Then looking over the top of her trifocals she asked me, "You *do* know where the book of Ecclesiastes is located, don't you?"

"Of course, Sarah," I answered, feigning offense. "Right after Second Moses."

"Hmm," she harrumphed. "Go on with your work, and I'll share this with you. Actually, it's going to be a quiz. As a physician, you should be able to interpret this passage."

She glanced skeptically over at me again. "But maybe not. We'll see."

Now curious, I once again began to gently repair her wound, waiting for her to continue. Lori hadn't left the room and was standing right behind me, listening.

"Now this is from the twelfth chapter," she began. "And the writer is describing the travails of old age. Let's start with this one, and you tell me what he's referring to. Keep in mind, Robert, he's contrasting the days of our youth with those as we grow old. 'Before the sun and the light and the moon and the stars grow dark, and the clouds return after the rain.'"

I thought for a moment, trying to shift into the mind of the writer. "He's talking about failing eyesight," I ventured. "Maybe even cataracts."

"Not bad," Sarah responded. "That's what I would think. Now, how about this. 'When the keepers of the house tremble, and the strong men stoop.'"

"That's too easy," I answered. "Bad balance would be my guess."

"And how about osteoporosis," she added. "With that stooping business."

I nodded and she went on. "'When the grinders cease because they are few.'"

"Grinders…" I mused. Then with sudden insight I said, "Oh, he's talking about teeth."

"Right," Sarah agreed. "Not many dentures back then. And 'When the doors to the street are closed and the sound of grinding fades.'"

I stopped and sat up straight again, puzzled by this one. *The doors of the street…* I didn't have a clue.

"Constipation!" Lori whispered in my ear.

Sarah heard and looked over at her and smiled. "That's exactly right," she remarked. "A little slow on that one, Robert," glancing back at me. "See, I told you these writers had a sense of humor."

Lori patted me on the shoulder and said, "A little slow there, Dr. Lesslie."

Sarah chuckled and continued. "You should be able to get this one, Robert, so pay attention. 'When people rise up at the sound of birds, but all their songs grow faint.'"

"Got it!" I exclaimed, jumping in. "It gets harder to sleep well as we get older, and the 'songs' refers to hearing loss."

"Uh-huh," Sarah agreed. "And all too true. Now this—'When people are afraid of heights and of dangers in the streets; when the almond tree blossoms and the grasshopper drags itself along.'"

"That must have something to do with losing your balance and falling," I ventured.

"And running into screen doors," Sarah quipped, looking down at her bleeding arm.

"And the grasshopper must refer to things like arthritis and bad knees and hips," I added. "But I don't know about the almond blossoms."

Sarah looked over to Lori, who was slowing shaking her head. "I don't know what that could be," the young nurse said.

"That one's not so easy," Sarah reassured her. "Most people think the pale almond blossoms refer to our hair becoming gray and white with old age."

"That makes sense," Lori agreed.

Sarah glanced over at me once more and without looking down at the page said, "And finally, Robert, 'Remember him—before the silver cord is severed, and the golden bowl is broken.'"

I was looking up at her now, struck by the peace evident on her face.

She closed her Bible and laid it down on the stretcher. Then with a twinkle in her eyes she said, "Now *that* is a hidden treasure."

Remember your Creator
in the days of your youth.

ECCLESIASTES 12:1

22

A Little Help from My Friends

Rob Flynn hurried to the desk and leaned over, almost into the face of Amy Connors.

"We need some stat lab work in 3!" he exclaimed. "And an EKG!"

Amy looked up at our newest and youngest ER doctor, backed away a little, and said, "Sure, Dr. Flynn. What do you want me to order?"

He hesitated a moment, rolled his eyes heavenward, then said, "The usual. And a blood gas too."

He was gone and back in room 3 before Amy could clarify "the usual" business.

She shook her head at me as I walked up, then picked up the phone and dialed the number for the lab.

"What's going on in 3?" I asked Lori Davidson. She had just walked out of the room and over to the nurses' station.

She started shaking her head as well, and grinning.

"Your young Dr. Flynn is off on another tangent," she said. "I tried to give him a little guidance, but he wouldn't listen."

"Guidance?" I asked. "About what?"

"There's a twenty-two-year-old woman in room 3 who says she took an overdose of pills. She's crying, almost hysterical, and Dr. Flynn immediately started ordering stuff. We've got two IVs going and she's on a cardiac monitor. Then he ran out here to order some lab studies."

"The *usual*," Amy interjected, rolling her eyes and spinning in her chair. "What am I supposed to do with that?"

"Nothing," Lori told her. "At least for the moment."

"What do you mean?" I asked. "Is the woman stable? Or suicidal?"

"She's fine," Lori said, still smiling and shaking her head. "I tried to tell him, but he was in a swivet and wasn't listening to anything I was saying."

"Tell him what?" I asked, glancing over to room 3 as one of our techs rolled the EKG machine in that direction.

"Well, before he got into the room, I asked the patient what she had taken and why," Lori explained. "She's upset with her boyfriend and wanted to get his attention. She's certainly not suicidal."

"But she still overdosed," I said. "And Rob needs to handle that, no matter how it happened."

"Dr. Lesslie, she took *two* penicillin tablets," Lori said flatly.

"Two!" Amy repeated, laughing.

"And she's not even allergic."

I stood there, absorbing what I had just heard.

"Someone needs to tell Dr. Flynn," I told them.

"You try," Lori said, walking around the counter. "You ER docs are a hardheaded bunch."

"Now don't count *me* in that group," I told her, feigning offense.

She stopped, looked straight in my eyes, put her hands on her hips, and raised her eyebrows.

And I remembered.

"Mr. Greaves, tell me when this started."

The fifty-year-old man was resting quietly in front of me on the stretcher in room 2. He had loosened his tie. His shirt was open, and his hands were folded over his bare chest, where I could see the electrodes for his cardiac telemetry. He was being routinely monitored at the nurses' station.

"I had the first episode yesterday, Dr. Lesslie," he began. "I was at work, in my office. Just sitting at my desk and things suddenly became dim—cloudy, and I felt as if I was going to pass out. It lasted only a few seconds and then was gone. No headache or chest pain, nothing. And I felt fine. Then the one this morning…"

He paused, took a deep breath, and blew it out slowly.

"That one *scared* me. I was in my office again, on the phone, and the next thing I knew I was on the floor with my secretary standing over me. I don't remember anything that happened."

"No headache with that one?" I asked. "Or any numbness or weakness?"

He started rubbing his right hand and forearm.

"Maybe some numbness here," he said, raising his hand just a little. "But I might have hit it or bruised it when I fell."

"Uh-huh," I murmured, making some notes on his chart.

"Anything else? Any other episodes like this or anything unusual in the past few days?"

He thought for a moment then shook his head. "I've been fine. I run every day, don't smoke, and have a glass of red wine in the evening, like the doctor ordered." He looked up and gave me a nervous smile.

His exam was completely normal, as were his vital signs. He seemed to be in great health.

"We'll need to do some tests," I told him. "I need to find out why you're having these spells."

I was turning to leave the room when he asked, "What do you think it is?"

Facing him again, I said, "The most likely thing is a TIA—transient ischemic attack. That would explain your symptoms, and it might be a warning sign for an impending stroke. That's what we need to find out, so we can make sure it doesn't happen."

"That's what I was afraid of," he sighed, staring down at his hands.

"But just relax. You're in the right place, and we're going to be sure you're okay."

At the nurses' station I turned to Amy Connors and said, "We need some blood work in 2, and then a stat MRI of his brain."

"What about an EKG?"

It was Lori Davidson, who was the nurse for Mr. Greaves. She had just walked up beside me.

"Yeah," I said, looking down at Amy again. "And an EKG."

Then I turned and faced Lori. "Why do you say an EKG?"

That would be part of a TIA workup and I should have ordered it, but her suggestion struck me as unusual.

"Don't you think it's cardiac?" she asked, looking up at me calmly.

I thought for a moment, then said, "Well, it could be. But no, it sounds like a classic TIA. He doesn't have any heart history or risk factors, other than being a man."

"I know, but I thought when I was taking his blood pressure I might have heard an extra beat or two. And I wonder if he's having an arrhythmia of some kind."

I studied her face for a moment, thinking. She was trying to be helpful, and I wasn't threatened or bothered by that. But I hadn't heard anything unusual when I listened to his chest. His heartbeat had been nice and regular.

"No, that's a thought, but it's not his heart," I said firmly, turning again to Amy. "You can get the EKG after he gets back from radiology."

"But Dr. Lesslie, something just doesn't seem right about that man. I have a gut feeling that—"

Spinning around to her I said, "Lori, listen, we'll *get* the EKG but—"

"V-tach! Room 2!"

It was Jeff Ryan. He had been sitting behind the desk watching the telemetry monitor and had seen it. I glanced over and there was the sawtooth pattern of this deadly rhythm. It wasn't stopping.

Lori and I bolted for room 2, and one of our techs raced to the crash cart in the hallway and started rolling it in our direction.

Mr. Greaves's eyes were wide with fear and his mouth gaped open. He was futilely trying to say something and his right hand was waving purposelessly in the air.

Then without warning—"No pulse!" Lori was standing at his side, her fingertips over his left carotid.

The crash cart rolled up beside me and I grabbed the paddles of the defibrillator.

"Mr. Greaves, you might feel this…"

His eyes were closed now. His arm had flopped to his side.

"All clear!" I called out.

We got him back, with only two faint red marks on his chest to show for his brush with death. He was alert, talking, thankful, and on his way to the cardiac care unit.

Lori and I were alone in room 2.

"Lori," I stammered. "I…should have listened. You were right about his heart. I just thought…"

This was her moment to say, "I told you so," and I was ready to accept it.

"Dr. Lesslie, it was just a gut feeling. And he's going to be fine."

Trust in the Lord with all your heart
and lean not on your own understanding;
in all your ways submit to him,
and he will make your paths straight.

Proverbs 3:5-6

23

DAVEY

Davey Mahaffey had a long and twisted road ahead of him, one filled with potholes and pain. We knew that early on, when he was only four years old.

His mother brought him to the ER late one December evening, complaining of fever, earache, and crying.

"He cried all last night, and we didn't get a lick of sleep," Kayla Mahaffey lamented, with an accusatory glare at her young son. She had a two-year-old on her hip and looked to be about six months pregnant with another child.

Davey sat alone on the stretcher, his shoeless feet dangling over the edge. His lower lip protruded—it trembled as he looked up at me, and his large brown eyes were wet with tears as he desperately tried to appear brave.

I glanced down at his chart, checking his vital signs once more.

Temp was 102 and his pulse and respirations were a little fast. *Probably the fever or the pain, or being scared, or all of the above.*

He was a pitiful sight, and I stepped over to him and gently put a hand on his shoulder.

"Tell me what the problem is tonight," I spoke to him, putting the clipboard on the counter and sitting down on the stretcher beside him.

He looked up at me and without a word pointed to his left ear. Then he glanced past me to where his mother stood, briefly caught her eye, and quickly stared down at the floor.

"Can't you talk?" his mother scolded. "Tell the doctor what's wrong!"

"That's okay," I said, not looking over at her but studying Davey. "It's *this* ear, right?"

He nodded as I reached out and gently touched the left side of his head.

It was an ear infection, and a bad one. The eardrum was tense, red, and bulging. Everything else—his throat, lungs, abdomen—was fine.

I explained to his mother what was going on and that I would write a prescription for an antibiotic and something for pain. Davey would need to be rechecked by his family doctor in a couple of days to be sure this infection was clearing.

"Any questions?" I asked her.

"Nope," was her terse and only response.

As I pulled the curtain of room 4 closed behind me, I heard her yell, "Stop it!" I had noticed the child on her hip becoming impatient and starting to squirm a little. Davey's mother had apparently exhausted her patience and was ready to get out of here. I quickly wrote the prescriptions, handed the chart to one of the nurses, and moved on to my next patient.

Two days later, Davey was back in the ER. It was late in the evening again, and this time his temperature was 103.

The triage nurse had again taken him to room 4. When I pulled back the curtain, I was greeted by a man standing in the far corner. His arms were folded across his chest and he was impatiently tapping his foot on the tiled floor.

"I'm Davey's father," he told me. "His mother's home with a headache, and so I'm here."

I was about to say something, when he added, "He's no better. Still runnin' fever and still whimperin' all the time."

The tone of his voice—frustrated and accusatory—caused me to pause and carefully study this young man. He was of medium height, maybe five-foot-ten, and slender. His hair was unkempt and he slouched a little. He was wearing faded blue jeans and a rumpled camouflage hunting jacket. When I looked over at him, he glanced down at his boy, unwilling to meet my eyes.

This time Davey was lying down on the stretcher with his hands folded across his belly. Those same big brown eyes looked up at me, but there was no sign of recognition, and he didn't move.

His exam was the same as the other night. His left eardrum was still red and bulging, and there was no sign of infection anywhere else. His neck was completely supple, which relieved me. There were no signs of meningitis.

The antibiotic I had written two days ago should have taken care of this problem. I wouldn't have expected his ear to be completely clear this quickly, but it should have been improving.

I explained this to his father. I told him we would need to be more aggressive this time, giving Davey an injection of an antibiotic and writing for a different medication.

"Well…" his father stammered. " You see…his mom and I thought he would get better on his own, since it was only an ear infection. And we didn't get the medicine."

They what? I was startled by this, and by how cavalier his statement was. And then I became angry.

"Mr. Mahaffey, your boy needed that medicine two days ago, and you—"

"Now hold on there, Doctor," he interrupted, still not looking at me and fumbling for something in one of his coat pockets.

"It's not like we're made of money," he continued. "We couldn't afford the medicine, and anyway, we thought he would get better on his own."

Now I was *really* getting angry. The antibiotic I had prescribed would cost less than $10, and the pain medicine not even that much.

I was about to tell him that when he apparently found what he was searching for in his pocket. He pulled out the rumpled prescription I had written two days earlier and started to unfold it. At the same time, two brand-new packs of cigarettes and three lottery tickets tumbled onto the stretcher. I reached over and picked up one of the tickets, looking for the date. Just as I suspected, these had been bought earlier today.

Mr. Mahaffey grabbed the cigarettes and tickets and stuffed them back in his pocket. Then he reached out for the ticket I was holding, and with his other hand, held out the prescription.

"Here," was all he would say.

I stared at it, shook my head, and then looked down at Davey. He was only four years old, and he depended on this man and his mother to take care of him, to look after him. Instead, they placed cigarettes and lottery tickets and who knows what else ahead of his health and well-being. Maybe ahead of his very life.

My body tensed, and I felt a hot flush spread across my face and down my neck. I knew I had to leave the room.

And the children of men
take refuge in the shadow of Your wings.

Psalm 36:7 nasb

24

THE OTHER SIDE OF THE COIN

D r. Lesslie, my sister is on her way to the ER and really wants to see you, if she can."

Lori Davidson had walked up behind me in the medicine room, where I was washing my hands.

"Sure, Lori," I told her, turning around and tossing the wet paper towels into a nearby trash can. "What's going on?"

"I think you've met her," she began. "Cindy Brockerman. She works up on one of the med-surg floors."

"Sure, I know Cindy," I told her.

Lori took a deep breath and sighed. I waited.

"Cindy and her husband have been trying for a long time to get pregnant—three or four years now. About two years ago they started going to a fertility doctor in Charlotte, and then a month and a half ago she finally became pregnant. As you can imagine, the whole family was excited."

She looked at me with troubled eyes and I nodded. I knew where this was heading.

"I think she's having a miscarriage," Lori said, her voice trembling as she looked away. "She started bleeding this afternoon and called her doctor. Since it's the weekend, their office is closed and he advised her to come here and be checked. She should be here any minute."

Lori grabbed a Kleenex from a box on the counter and dried her eyes.

"I don't know what she'll do if they lose this baby," she said quietly, shaking her head. "They tried so hard for so long, and I..."

The tears choked her words as she slumped onto a stool in the corner of the room.

"Let's wait and see what's going on," I said. "Maybe it's something simple and there's no real problem."

She nodded her head but didn't look up.

As soon as Cindy came through triage, she was led back to the GYN room.

"I'll help you with this one," Virginia Granger said, standing across the nurses' station from me. "Lori doesn't need to be back there. Not just yet, not until we find out what's going on."

She was right, and I appreciated her help.

Cindy was lying comfortably on the stretcher as Virginia and I entered. Her husband was standing beside her, holding her hand. He looked up at us as Virginia closed the door.

"Hey, Dr. Lesslie," Cindy said, her voice quiet and trembling. "This is my husband, Tim."

"Good to meet you, Tim," I said, shaking his hand. Then I looked down at Cindy and put a hand on her shoulder. "Tell me what's going on."

Lori's fears were confirmed. Cindy was having a miscarriage and had probably already lost the baby. We would be sending her upstairs to see one of the staff obstetricians.

I left the shattered couple in the room with Virginia and went up the hallway to find Lori. I needed to tell her, and she needed to be with her sister.

An hour later, Virginia and I were standing alone at the nurses' station.

"That's such a hard thing," she said. "They're devastated, and so is Lori. I just don't know how best to help them."

I didn't either.

I was about to say something, when the triage nurse walked up and quietly slid the clipboard of room 3 across the counter to me. Glancing down, I read the chief complaint.

"Twenty-year-old female—*panic attacks.*"

"She's fine," the nurse told me. "This has been going on for a couple of months and she decided to come in now and get something for them."

"You go do that," Virginia told me, nodding at the chart. "And I'll go check on Lori."

As I pulled the curtain of room 3 aside, I was assaulted by the stench of stale cigarette smoke. It clung to the clothing of the slender young woman sitting on the stretcher, her legs crossed and her head tilted backward. Her mouth was open as she loudly and aggressively chewed gum. Behind her stood a young man. His curly black hair hung haphazardly over his shoulders and over one side of his face. His eyes were closed as he massaged the girl's neck.

"Excuse me," I said, pulling the curtain closed behind me and looking down at the chart once more. "I'm Dr. Lesslie. What can we do for you this afternoon, Ms. Talford?"

Renee Talford slowly sat up and looked at me. Her eyes were dull and she was swaying a little. Or maybe it was the guy behind her, moving her from side to side as he continued to rub her neck and shoulders. His eyes were still closed.

I glanced again at her record to see if she was taking any medication, something that might explain her lack of alertness. Nothing.

"I've been having panic attacks," she began to explain. "They started a couple of months ago and are getting worse. I need something to take for them."

"Something strong," the man behind her mumbled.

"Do you have any medical problems?" I asked her. "Are you taking any medicine?"

"No, I don't have any problems," she listlessly replied. "And they told me I was fine when I went to the ER in Lancaster."

"When was that?" I asked. "And what did they—"

"Two weeks ago," she interrupted. "They did a bunch of tests and said everything was normal and they couldn't explain why I was having the attacks. But they didn't give me anything. That's why we're here."

"She needs something strong," the phantom behind her mumbled again.

I was growing impatient. Her vital signs were completely normal, and a brief physical exam didn't offer any explanation for her panic attacks. She seemed to be in good health, and she seemed to be calm.

I asked her about any signs or symptoms of depression, and whether she had ever thought about hurting herself.

"Of course not," she responded. "I just need something for my nerves. When I get these attacks, I start shaking all over and sweating, and I have trouble breathing. I took one of my mother's Valiums once and it helped. Maybe something like that."

"We don't usually prescribe Valium in the ER for panic attacks," I explained. "But there are some effective medicines we can try, and at the same time get you lined up with one of the mental-health clinics here in town."

This opened the eyes of her boyfriend and he looked at me and said, "Listen, Doctor. She just needs something for her nerves, something to help her relax."

I struggled not to respond to that, but I needed a little more information from Renee before I decided on the most appropriate medicine to offer her.

"Is there any chance you're pregnant?" I asked. This was important, because if she were, that would rule out the use of several classes of drugs.

"Yes," she answered flatly.

"Yes, there's a chance?" I asked.

"No," she snipped. "Yes, I'm pregnant."

Her boyfriend chuckled and kept rubbing her neck.

"How far along do you think you are?" I asked her, my impatience growing.

"It doesn't matter," she told me. "We're going to a clinic in Columbia tomorrow and have a procedure."

A procedure?

"You mean an abortion?" I asked.

"Yeah," her boyfriend answered. "It's just not a good time for this right now."

I looked at him and then at Renee. She was nodding her head and chewing her gum.

Not a good time for this.

I thought of Cindy Brockerman and her husband, and without a word I left the room.

This day I call the heavens and the earth
as witnesses against you
that I have set before you life and death,
blessings and curses.
Now choose life,
so that you and your children may live
and that you may love the LORD your God,
listen to his voice,
and hold fast to him.

Deuteronomy 30:19-20

25

SAM'S

They say if you stand long enough at the only street corner in the beach town of Garden City, South Carolina, right out in front of Sam's Restaurant, you will eventually see everyone you've ever known. I can't vouch for that, but I *can* say that it sometimes seems the ER is that kind of place.

"Doc, you any kin to Pete Lesslie?"

It was a Saturday afternoon and I was splinting the sprained wrist of a fifty-year-old softball player who was visiting from Knoxville and playing in a regional tournament. He had slid into second base, was tagged out by about three feet, and had come away with only a swollen and painful wrist to show for his efforts.

I glanced at his record again, noticed where he was from, and made the connection. My older brother, Peter, and his family have lived in the Knoxville area for more than forty years.

"Yes, I have a brother in Knoxville," I answered, putting the last touches on his splint.

"Great guy!" he told me, smiling. "Coached my two boys in T-ball years ago, and was always one of their favorites. Great guy. Small world, isn't it?"

A few weeks after that, I was taking care of an older woman with a significant burn of her left forearm. She was traveling through on her way to Florida and had spilled hot water from the coffeemaker in her hotel room.

As I cleaned and dressed the wound, I asked her where she was from.

"New Brunswick," she answered, her Canadian accent strong and easily identifiable.

I asked what part, and when she said, "Saint John," I looked up at her with renewed interest.

"We have family in Saint John," I said. "Or at least we used to."

I told her of our annual summer trips to Nova Scotia when I was a boy.

We would visit relatives along the way and ultimately make it to Sandy Cove, the home of my mother's parents.

"We would always stop and spend a night or two in Saint John with a great-aunt and great-uncle," I went on. Then I shared a story that had been indelibly burned into my young and impressionable psyche. I had been twelve years old at the time, and the episode was one of the most humbling in my memory.

My parents had recently taught me how to play bridge, and not lacking confidence, I thought I was pretty good at the game. Some cousins, Dan and his wife, Phyllis, had joined the family for dinner. During some casual conversation, Dan brought up playing bridge and I seized on it. My older brother, Peter, was there and I challenged Dan and Phyllis to a match with the two of us. I remember they were a little reluctant, but I was brash and insistent. I think Peter was reluctant too, but he humored me and the four of us sat down to play.

We were skunked. No, not skunked. We were annihilated. Peter just smiled and took his medicine, but I limped away from the table, with my tail between my legs.

My Canadian patient suddenly burst out laughing as I finished my story.

"What's so funny?" I asked her.

"Were they Dan and Phyllis Turnbridge?" she asked me, still smiling.

"Yes, that's right!" I answered, wondering how she knew the names of my relatives.

She chuckled again and said, "Dr. Lesslie, Dan and Phyllis have been friends of ours for years, and we play bridge every Thursday evening."

She paused, her eyes still twinkling.

"And you needn't have felt so bad about their beating you and your brother," she continued. "You see, Dan and Phyllis are professional bridge players—champions—and have been since before you were born."

"What?" I stammered, trying to put all of this together.

"That's right," she said. "Champions."

And if *that* didn't prove how small a world we live in, a late-night visitor to the ER would soon hammer the point home.

It was a little after midnight, and a minor accident had occurred out on I-77. EMS brought in three patients to be examined, all on their way home from a meeting in Columbia. They had been heading north, and another vehicle had failed to yield as they entered the highway, forcing these three women into the median and causing them to spin around several times.

Fortunately, no one was seriously injured. I was examining the last of them, a sixty-eight-year-old woman who, I happened to note, lived in Mount Holly. That was a small town just north of Charlotte, where I had grown up.

When I told her this, her brow furrowed and she seemed to be concentrating on something. Then her eyes opened wide and she stared at me with a sudden realization.

"Dr. Lesslie!" she exclaimed. "You must be Robert Lesslie! And your father is Thomas Lesslie."

"That's right," I told her, struggling to recognize this woman.

"We went to the same church in Mount Holly," she went on. "And I sang in the choir with your mother, Harriett. Sat right beside her."

I still wasn't quite able to place this woman, but admittedly it had been more than thirty years. I glanced again at her chart and checked her name once more.

"Yes, Mrs. Abernathy, Momma sang alto in the choir for a lot of years," I told her.

"Of course she did," she replied knowingly. "And I remember you and your father and sisters sitting a couple of rows back on the left side of the church."

She was right. That was where we sat each Sunday.

"And I remember your mother getting so angry," she continued, causing me to stop what I was doing and look at her again.

"That's right," she added, pointing a finger in my face. "You were a holy terror, and it was all your father could do to keep you seated in that pew. And when the communion plate would come by, you would—"

"I think you're going to be okay, Mrs. Abernathy," I interrupted her. One of our nurses was on the other side of the curtain and I could hear her giggling. It was time to bring this visit to a close.

"Well, I'm just glad to see you made something of yourself," she said, straightening herself and getting up from the stretcher. "There were more than a few of us who wondered about that."

This brought laughter from behind the curtain, and that was all I needed.

"We'll be letting you get home," I told her, easing my way to the door. "And tell everyone in Mount Holly hello for me."

There's a lesson here somewhere. Clearly it *is* a small world, and you have to be careful about standing in any one place for very long. But maybe more significantly:

And be sure your sin
will find you out.

Numbers 32:23 nkjv

26

Make Me an Instrument

Lori Davidson walked out of room 4, shaking her head with a troubled look on her face.

"What's going on?" I asked her, curious.

She walked up beside me at the nurses' station and just stood there for a moment, silent.

Then she looked up at me and said, "The man in room 4, Mr. Nelson."

I glanced down at the chart in front of me, the one belonging to room 4—Brian Nelson.

"This guy?" I asked, tapping the clipboard. "With the sore throat?"

I was a little confused about him. He had come into the ER with several vague complaints, finally settling on a painful throat. His exam had been completely normal, and I had recommended some over-the-counter medication.

"Is there a problem?" I glanced down at his chart again, studying his vital signs, second-guessing myself. *What had I missed?*

"No, there's not a problem," Lori reassured me. "At least not a medical one."

What did that mean?

She took a deep breath as if trying to collect her thoughts.

"Every morning on the drive into work," she began, "I say a little prayer. Something very simple, and it's always the same thing. I pray for patience and a cool head. And then sometimes I pray for someone to cross my path who needs more than just medical care. I'll ask the Lord for that discernment and to give me a chance to share my faith, and to reach out to someone who really needs a word, or maybe just a smile and a pat on the shoulder. I guess it's a chance to be an instrument that I pray for."

She chuckled a little, and seemed to blush.

"I've learned not to pray that prayer unless I mean business," she explained. "Unless I'm ready to step up, 'cause the Lord will always send someone. He's going to put someone right in front of me and see if I was serious."

I glanced over at the closed curtain of room 4. "So, tell me about Brian Nelson," I said to her, sliding his chart to one side and leaning against the countertop. "It wasn't just a sore throat, was it?"

"No, it wasn't," she answered quietly. "I had gone into the room with his discharge instructions and was about to lead him out when I noticed something. It was just a little thing really, but as I had been talking with him, his shoulders seemed to slump a little and he looked down at the floor. But only for a second. Then he was standing up as if nothing had happened."

"You thought that was unusual?" I asked her. I probably wouldn't have noticed such a small thing, and would have been focused on sending him out to the waiting room and taking care of our next patient. That realization suddenly made me feel uncomfortable—and a little guilty.

"It was unusual for *him*," she said without hesitation. "He was in control the whole time he was here, upbeat and everything. Even though he wasn't exactly clear on what had brought him to the ER."

She was right about that. All of his complaints were vague, not really significant, and yet…

"I stopped in the doorway and walked back over to him," she continued. "I just stood there for a minute, looking at him. All I said was 'Mr. Nelson,' and then I just waited. It must have been the way I said it, I guess. We just looked at each other and then he started talking. No, *unloading* is more like it. He really needed to share what was on his heart, but he didn't know how. And he had no one else to talk to. I guess that's why he came here."

Lori looked over at me and shook her head.

"The amount of pain and hurt we see—not the physical kind, but the pain in a person's heart—sometimes it's just beneath the surface. And I wonder how some of them make it, with the things they're dealing with."

She paused, and there was that troubled look again.

"You remember a wreck out on Highway 21 about six months ago?" she continued. "A pulpwood truck crossed the median and hit an SUV with a family in it. Mother, father, and two young children. Only the father survived."

I was struggling to remember this particular accident, we see so many—

Suddenly I stood up and looked over at room 4. Then I glanced back at Lori.

"You mean he...Brian Nelson..." I stammered.

"He's the father," Lori said, almost whispering. "He blames himself. He doesn't understand why he's still alive and his family is...You need to go talk to him, Dr. Lesslie. He needs some help."

Of course he did. How had I missed that? Why didn't I *see*?

If Lori hadn't been listening with her heart and not her ears and hadn't picked up on the real reason Brian Nelson was in the ER, I would have just sent him on his way. And then what? And how many others like Brian Nelson had I overlooked? How many real but unspoken needs?

She must have seen the perplexed look on my face, and she stepped a little closer. Quietly she said, "The Lord always answers that prayer, about asking him to put someone in your path. You just need to be ready."

It is only with the heart that one can see rightly;
what is essential is invisible to the eye.

ANTOINE DE SAINT-EXUPÉRY (1900–1944)

27

COACH D

"You know who that is, don't you?" Amy Connors whispered to me over the counter.

I was standing at the nurses' station, making some notes on the chart of the little girl in cardiac.

Amy was nodding toward someone behind me. I turned just in time to see our triage nurse lead a man through the door of the cardiac room. He was huge—at least six-foot-six—and was built like a mountain. He disappeared and I turned back to Amy.

"No, I didn't see his face. Who is he?" I asked, resuming my charting.

"That's Coach Devereux," she answered, her voice quiet, almost reverent.

I had heard of Joe Devereux but had never met the man. He was a legend in this part of the upstate, having taken one of the area high-school football teams to the state championship six times and winning five of them.

"I bet that's his granddaughter in cardiac," she added.

I glanced at the top of the chart in front of me, searching for the patient's name.

Cindy Devereux. That's not a common name around here. Amy must be right.

Jeff Ryan was walking up the hallway from the back of the department. He had been on break and was just now returning. "Is that who I think it is?" he asked.

"Yeah, that was Coach D," Amy answered. "He must be with the little girl in cardiac."

Jeff walked over beside me, leaned heavily on the countertop with his forearms, and said, "My older brother played football for him—starting linebacker for three years. You should hear some of the stories he tells about him."

"Like what?" Amy asked, her voice rising a little as she leaned in closer.

"Well, for one thing, what they say about him being so strong is all true," Jeff said, nodding. "He's an ex-marine, you know, and tough as nails. I saw him bench press more than three hundred pounds one day during gym."

"My cousin saw him bench press two tackles and a safety!" Amy volunteered excitedly. "And I heard he picked up the back end of a VW so one of his players could change a tire!"

"Now wait just a minute," I interrupted. "Two tackles and a safety? That's three football players. And he picked up a Volkswagen?"

"That's what they say," Amy said, her voice firm and her eyes narrowing in my direction.

"And it's all true," a voice spoke behind us.

It was Virginia Granger, our head nurse, and she had just walked up. We turned and looked at her.

"He's older now, of course," Virginia continued. "Retired two years ago, I think. And he probably couldn't lift that much anymore."

"Still looks pretty strong to me," Amy opined.

"You sound like you know him," Jeff said to Virginia. "What's he like?"

She glanced over at the closed cardiac room door and then back to us.

"He's tough as nails," she answered. "Just like you said, Jeff. But every kid who played for Coach D would do anything for him. He changed lives and taught his players a lot of things, like respect, and sacrifice, and loyalty."

"Some people think he's...well...that he's mean," Jeff said, glancing back over his shoulder. "They say you can't talk to him."

Virginia chuckled and said, "Some people say the same things about me."

She was looking directly over her bifocals at Jeff, who quickly looked away as his face turned a flaming red.

"No, he's not mean," she went on. "But I can understand why people might think that. He's just quiet, and only speaks when he has something important to say."

"Unless he's on the sidelines at a football game," Amy interjected. "And then he has *plenty* to say."

Virginia didn't respond to this comment and continued.

"He's been through a lot. His oldest boy developed leukemia at the age of twelve and really suffered for a couple of years before he died. That really hit Joe hard, and he was never the same. He became even more quiet and withdrawn. All business, I guess you would say. But he still took care of his players, and his family. He has another son and two daughters, and they all live nearby. That's been a good thing for him."

"Wow," Amy whispered. "I just thought he was…like you said, all business. When I was in high school, I don't think I ever saw him smile."

"You probably didn't," Virginia sighed. "But that doesn't make him mean. Sad, maybe, but not mean. When you lose one of your children, it's hard *not* to shut down the warm and trusting side of you."

She looked down at the chart in front of me and asked, "How is Cindy? She looked pretty sick when she came in."

"She's got a bad pneumonia," I told her. "With one side of her chest almost completely socked in. But she's breathing better now, and should be alright."

"That little girl has been a blessing for Joe Devereux," Virginia said quietly. "She's been just what he needed, a real gift. She's what, five years old? And she's his only grandchild. Since she was born, Joe seems to be opening up again. And I've even seem him smile a couple of times," she added, winking at Amy. "So don't be too hard on him."

Then she glanced back at cardiac again and sighed.

"I can only imagine how worried he is right now."

I stepped back from the counter and said, "I'll go check on him, and make sure he's okay."

The door of cardiac closed quietly behind me and I stepped into the room.

On the other side of the stretcher stood one of our nurses, adjusting the rate of the IV fluids. She looked up at me and nodded, reassuring me with a smile.

Cindy seemed to be sleeping quietly on the bed, the IV tubing taped to her left arm and an oxygen mask securely attached to her face. Her color was better now, and she was no longer struggling for breath.

I looked down, and there was Joe Devereux. Coach D. This huge man was on his knees, hanging his head into his left hand. His other enormous arm rested on the side of the stretcher as he gently stroked the cheek of his granddaughter.

He looked up at me—and his face was not that of a rugged, indomitable football coach. Instead I saw in his eyes fear and helplessness. And a question.

"She's going to be alright," I quietly told him. "She's going to be fine."

His face softened and an enormous sob escaped his giant frame. He leaned close to his granddaughter and whispered something in her ear. I couldn't hear what he said, but she smiled weakly up at him and slowly raised her arm and laid her tiny hand on his.

What he did next made me stop what I was doing. He was singing quietly to her. It was a familiar lullaby and I could just make out the words.

Sleep, my child, and peace attend thee,
All through the night.
Guardian angels God will send thee,
All through the night.

SIR HAROLD BOULTON (1859–1935)

28

180—AND A NEW DIRECTION

hy me? What did I ever do to deserve this?
    Jennifer Conley was twenty-six years old. The question had been simmering in her heart for a dozen years, and now it was boiling over. As she was driving to Rock Hill General for her overnight shift in the ER it finally took the form of uttered words. At first they were quiet, subdued, and barely audible. But soon, alone in the car, she was yelling, clutching the steering wheel as tightly as she could.

Why me? Lord, tell me what I've done...

At the age of ten, Jennifer had started losing weight. Her parents had noticed it, but it didn't make sense. She was eating more than ever and always seemed hungry. When they took her to their family doctor, it was a simple diagnosis. And the words would forever change her life and the lives of her parents.

"Jennifer has diabetes," Dr. Jones had told them. "Her blood sugar is sky-high, and probably has been for quite a while. We'll need to start her on insulin right away and get this under control."

Her parents were stunned. They just stared at each other and then at their daughter.

"But for how long?" Jennifer's father finally asked. "Just a couple of weeks, and then some pills? Or maybe we just have to be real careful with her diet?"

"I'm afraid not," their doctor answered. "At her age and with this level of blood sugar, I think she'll be on insulin the rest of her life."

Dr. Jones had been right. Jennifer had been started on insulin that afternoon and had been on it ever since. It had saved her life, and she had somehow been able to avoid the complications associated with this dreaded and complex disease.

Maybe it was the fear of those complications that had caused her outburst this morning. She was an ER nurse and had too often seen the ravages of advanced or poorly treated diabetes. It was a common problem in the emergency department. Just yesterday she had helped take care of a twenty-eight-year-old mother of two with a fifteen-year history of insulin-dependent diabetes. She had come in with renal failure, and within an hour she was in the dialysis unit. Her kidneys had been destroyed by the disease. She and her young family were looking at a bleak and frightening future.

Or maybe it was her own blood sugar this morning that had tipped the balance of her usually calm and controlled spirit. The meter had read 180. It was a number she hadn't seen in years, and she had tried to determine why it had gone up so high. She was always careful about her medicine, and about her diet and exercise.

Why me?

Jennifer was suddenly sobbing, and had to wipe her eyes with the back of her hand as she found a place in the parking lot.

She turned off her car and just sat there, drying her tears with a Kleenex.

Why...

She wasn't yelling anymore, and the word had barely crossed her lips when something silenced her. She leaned back in her seat and listened.

There it was again. It was a voice, clear and distinct, and it was speaking to her. The words she heard were unmistakable and were uttered with love and reassurance.

"My grace is sufficient for you."

Jennifer was overwhelmed by the real and loving presence of her Lord, and she was suddenly at peace. That moment and those words would forever be with her. Gone was the fear and anger that had crept into her heart.

Now, some twenty years later, Jennifer Conley is a nurse practitioner, specializing in the care of patients with diabetes. She has become the area's foremost educator for people with the disease she shares with them. Her confidence and faith have been a blessing for many—and she remains undaunted in her determination to live *with* this problem and not be controlled *by* it. His grace *is* sufficient.

It was that determination I saw in her eyes as she told me this story.

But it was more than that. There was a calm assurance there as well as she said, "Robert, the Lord has placed a hedge around me and protected me. I know there will be difficult days ahead, but we will handle it. Together, we will handle it."

My grace is sufficient for you,
for my power
is made perfect in your weakness.

2 CORINTHIANS 12:9

29

A Light in the Darkness

Raymond Jackson's lip was slowly coming back together. The laceration was a bad one, through-and-through and starting just below his nose.

"You'll need to see your dentist about this cracked tooth," I told him, tying knots in the last suture.

He nodded silently, his eyes still closed.

I leaned back on the stool, stretched my tight and aching back, and said, "Raymond, this is going to do fine, but you'll need to keep some ice on it and keep it clean."

"Call me Ray," he said, wincing as his mouth formed the words. "Everybody does."

"Okay, Ray. And we'll need to take these stitches out in six or seven days. Just don't trip on any more lamp cords."

His eyes squinted a little and his brow furrowed. I paused for a moment. *Isn't that how he told me this had happened? He had tripped on a cord in his living room, fallen, and struck his lip on the corner of a piece of furniture.*

Ray quickly glanced away, and when he turned back to me there was a smile on his face.

"Don't worry," he mumbled, his swollen lip barely moving. "I'll be careful."

I studied the seventy-year old man for a moment, not sure if I should pursue this. Something wasn't quite right. But he was sitting up now and swinging his legs over the edge of the stretcher.

"Six or seven days," he repeated my instructions. "Thanks, Dr. Lesslie."

He patted his thinning, wispy gray hair back into place, sighed as he looked down at his bloodstained plaid flannel shirt, then turned to the door and walked out into the hallway.

I didn't see Ray Jackson for another year or so. It was a Thursday evening, and Lori had brought him back through triage and straight to the ortho room. As he walked by the nurses' station I noticed he was holding his right arm bent at the elbow and tight against his chest. He nodded when he saw me.

"We need some labs on the child in 4," I told our secretary, sliding the clipboard across the countertop.

Lori walked back up and handed me Ray's chart.

"Looks like he broke his forearm," she told me. "And he hasn't said anything, but he needs something for pain."

"That bad?" I asked her, looking down at his record.

"It's pretty crooked, and almost poking through the skin."

She turned and headed back out to triage.

Ray was sitting on one of the stretchers in ortho, his feet dangling over the edge.

"Mr. Jackson," I said, walking over to him and shaking his good hand. "What did you do to yourself this time?"

"It's Ray, remember?" he teased. Then looking down at his injured arm he said, "I fell in the garage and must have landed on a step. I think it's broken."

It didn't take much of an exam to determine he was right. And so was Lori. The fractured end of one of the bones in his forearm was tenting the skin, almost breaking through. That was a narrowly avoided disaster.

I took a pillow from a nearby cabinet and carefully placed it under his arm, trying to give him some support and relief.

"Let's try this," I said. "And we'll get you something for pain. Then we'll need some X-rays."

With a smile on his face, he sighed and let his arm sink down into the pillow.

"Thanks, Doctor."

"Oh, and let's take a look at that lip," remembering his previous ER visit.

I leaned close and inspected my handiwork. *Not too bad.* The wound had healed nicely, with barely a scar. He smiled, and I noticed his cracked tooth hadn't been repaired.

"You did a good job," he told me.

"We've just got to keep you from falling down."

It wasn't too long before the radiology tech brought his X-rays back to the nurses' station and handed them to me. As I snapped them into place on the view box I heard a soft whistle behind me.

"That doesn't look so good."

I turned around to see Jimmy Wilson, an officer with the city police. Beside him stood an obviously inebriated young man in blue jeans, T-shirt, and handcuffs.

"There's a bed open back in ortho," Lori told Wilson. "Just a minor auto accident, right?"

"Yeah, he's fine," the officer replied. "Just need to have him checked out before I take him downtown."

They headed down the hallway while I put the X-rays back in their jacket and made some notes on Ray Jackson's chart. It was a bad injury, and a little unusual. He had broken the middle part of his ulna, something difficult to do with a simple fall. But I supposed if he'd struck it against the edge of a step...

Ray was back on his stretcher and talking with the police officer, who was now standing near the doorway. The handcuffed patient was lying on the other stretcher in the room and seemed to be enjoying a nap.

I told Ray about his injury, and that an orthopedist would need to be called in to take care of it. I mentioned that surgery might be needed.

"Oh, let's not do that," Ray sighed. "I've got things I need to be doing."

"The most important thing you need to be doing is getting that arm fixed," I gently but firmly told him.

"Listen to the doctor, Ray," the police officer said, reinforcing my words. "You don't want to get into any trouble with that arm."

Ray looked over at him and smiled.

Later, as I stood at the nurses' station waiting on the call from the orthopedist, Jimmy Wilson walked up.

"You know who that is, don't you, Doc? I mean, what he does?"

Turning to face the officer I said, "I know he's Ray Jackson, but that's about it. We've seen him here in the ER a few times. Why? What does he do?"

"I would bet he usually comes in with some kind of injury," he told me, putting his notebook on the countertop and then leaning his elbow on it. "Just like tonight."

I remembered his busted lip, and now this. "What's the connection?"

"After his wife died, Ray moved downtown into a tough area. He boards ten or twelve boys. They've all been in some kind of trouble—rough kids, all of 'em headed for bad trouble. But he works with them, makes sure they're in school, and sees to it they stay out of trouble. Problem is, it's a bad neighborhood, like I said, and we've got some people who see Ray as an easy mark. They must think he has some money or something. Every once in a while someone will break into his house and mess him up. I bet that's what happened tonight. I doubt if he fell in his garage. Heck, Doc, he doesn't *have* a garage."

It all made sense now—the busted lip, and now the fractured forearm. It was a defensive wound from holding up his arm trying to protect his face. Someone had been swinging a baseball bat or golf club.

"I'm going to talk with him again," I told Jimmy, turning and quickly striding down the hallway.

"Good luck with that!" he called after me.

I confronted Ray with this new information. His shoulders slumped and he hung his head with a sigh but didn't say anything.

"We need to get Jimmy involved," I told him. "We need to find the guys who did this."

He straightened and looked up at me.

"I know the guys who did this," he said calmly. "But I'm not going to press charges. Have you heard from the orthopedist?"

I looked at the man and saw the determination in his face.

"Ray—"

"Doc, I've got work to do."

The light shines in the darkness,
and the darkness has not overcome it.

JOHN 1:5

30

Tick-Tock

Wait! This can't be! There must be a mistake!
One of my partners and I were attending a medical conference in Atlanta. We were sitting at one of the front tables in the hotel's large convention room, awaiting the arrival of a well-known motivational speaker. He was a general surgeon, but more notably he had been a college and then pro basketball star. I had been looking forward to hearing him speak for months.

Off to our right, a scattering of applause began to crescendo, and we turned in our seats, craning our necks to identify the object of this attention.

It was the main speaker—at least I thought it was—and he was slowly making his way down one of the aisles.

A bit shocked, I quickly picked up the brochure lying on the table in front of me and checked the schedule for the evening. My index finger scanned down the page, and there it was. *Barry Settlemeyer.* It wasn't a mistake. It *was* him. I put the brochure back down on the table and joined in the applause that greeted this man as he approached the podium. He was only yards away now and I studied him closely, still perplexed and a little shaken.

When I was ten years old, Barry had been finishing his last year in college basketball at one of the schools in North Carolina. He was a star, and was widely admired not only for his physical ability and picture-perfect jump shot, but also for his kind and always calm demeanor. He was a role model, back when we still had those.

A stellar eight-year NBA career ended with a devastating knee injury, and he seemed to drop off the sports world's radar. I was in college myself by then, with a lot of things on my mind.

Through the years I would occasionally be reminded of Barry

Settlemeyer and of his jump shot and his character. Something would come up on TV or in conversation, and I would immediately be taken back to my memories of him when I was ten. Later I learned that he had gone to medical school after his years in pro basketball and had become a general surgeon. In fact, he was practicing in a city not very far from Rock Hill.

One day I saw his name on a flyer for a medical meeting and became determined to hear him speak. I might even be able to shake his hand and tell him I had been one of his biggest fans. I felt like a kid again. This was one of the real heroes of my youth.

Now, here he was right in front of me, stepping up to the podium and preparing to speak.

What had I been expecting? Who *had I been expecting?*

The shock had been immediate, and I still stared in disbelief, struggling for a moment to understand my response.

I suppose I'd been expecting to see the same tall, redheaded twenty-or-so-year-old energetically bouncing up the steps of the stage. Maybe he would be wearing a three-piece suit rather than a basketball uniform, but it would be the Barry Settlemeyer of my memory, of my youth.

But it wasn't.

Standing no more than fifteen feet from me was a tall, slender, aging gentleman, slightly stooped over. His hair was certainly not red any more, but gray and thinning. He fumbled for something in his coat pocket, then took out his bifocals and put them on. For a moment he focused on the notes spread out on the lectern in front of him.

It was Barry Settlemeyer, to be sure. I could see the same strong facial features, the same kind smile and warm eyes. And there were those same long, graceful fingers that had launched so many unbelievable jump shots. But he was different. He was…he was so much older.

How had this happened?

In my head I knew the answer. It just took my heart a few minutes to catch up. It was still Barry Settlemeyer, but changed now by the passage of time—thirty-five years of time.

Where had those years gone? I knew that time passes—the clock never stops ticking, but still…

I looked away from the man on the podium and struggled with these thoughts. Glancing down, I became aware of the freckles on the backs of my hands. And almost instantly I realized they weren't freckles. They were age spots.

Time is free, but it's priceless.
You can't own it, but you can use it.
You can't keep it, but you can spend it.
Once you've lost it,
you can never get it back.

HARVEY MACKAY (1932–)

31

A GATHERING OF VULTURES

A sudden movement off to the left of my car grabbed my attention. It was a pair of buzzards gracelessly landing in a grassy area just off the highway. Passing quickly, I had just enough time to see a half-dozen of the birds on the ground and the carcass of what seemed to be a deer. And I thought of Jonas Griffin.

"Dr. Lesslie, we need you in cardiac."

It was Lori Davidson, and there was unmistakable urgency in her voice.

Without saying anything else, she turned and hurried back into the room. I quickly followed.

"What's going on?" I asked her, walking over to the stretcher.

Lying in front of me was an elderly gentleman, probably in his nineties. His mouth was open and he was quietly snoring.

"He was just brought in from a nursing home," she answered, checking his blood pressure. "80 over 40," she told me, making a quick note on the palm of her hand. "The staff there thinks he might have had a stroke."

I noticed an unfamiliar nurse standing in the corner of the room, holding a clipboard tightly against her chest.

"I'm Sue Mills," she informed me. "I work out at the Manor, and this is one of my patients. Jonas Griffin. He was doing fine earlier this evening, and then I found him like this about an hour ago. We couldn't wake him up and so we called 9-1-1."

"Any medical problems?" I asked her, turning again to Mr. Griffin. "Medications?"

I tried to elicit some response from him. Nothing.

"Just some high blood pressure," the nurse answered. "And the only medicine he takes is lisinopril, 20 milligrams."

"No diabetes? Heart trouble? Nothing else?" I asked while checking his pupils. They were small and didn't react to light. The nursing home staff had been right—it looked like the diagnosis was going to be a stroke.

"No. Like I said, Jonas has been doing really well to be eighty-nine years old," she responded.

A CT scan of his head confirmed our suspicions—Mr. Griffin had suffered a significant bleed and was already showing evidence of increased pressure in his brain. There was nothing surgical to be done, and the best we could do for him was to get him upstairs and into a bed. He wasn't going to wake up from this.

"Any family?" I asked Sue Mills.

"He has some here in town, and some in Charlotte," she told me. "They've been called and should be here any time now."

"Fine," I said. "Let me know when they get here and I'll be glad to tell them what's going on with Mr. Griffin."

It was going to take a few hours to get a bed in the ICU, and I had other patients to see. I left Sue in the room with Mr. Griffin and Lori and went back out into the department.

An hour and a half later, Lori walked up to me and said, "The family is in cardiac with Mr. Griffin. I told them you would be in, and..." She paused.

I looked up from the chart in front of me and said, "And?"

There was an uncomfortable look on her face and she began to slowly shake her head. "It's a little awkward in there. You'll see." Then she turned and walked over to the medicine room.

Awkward? What did that mean?

I walked into the cardiac room, crowded with eight or nine people standing around Jonas's stretcher or leaning against the counter. They all looked over at me as I entered and closed the door.

"I'm Dr. Lesslie," I began. Then I informed them of Jonas's diagnosis, and his grim outlook. I waited for questions.

"I'm one of his sons," a distinguished-looking man said, walking over and shaking my hand. "Thank you for taking care of our father," he added. Then waving expansively behind him he said, "And these are assorted children and nephews and nieces. I won't bother to introduce them all to you."

Lori was right. This *was* a little awkward. But it soon got a lot worse.

"Now, Dr. Lesslie," the man said, stepping close and leaning into me, close enough to be uncomfortable. He glanced down at his wrist, adjusted his watch so he could determine the time, then looked up and asked, "How much longer do you think he has? Are we talking minutes or hours? Or…" and I was sure there was a note of exasperation in his voice, "days?"

Everyone behind him seemed to lean in my direction, straining to hear my answer and not wanting to miss it.

I felt my face begin to flush, and I studied those around me. There seemed to be a lot of concern here, but not for Jonas Griffin.

"I really can't say," I told them honestly, but bluntly. "It's impossible to know."

I was turning to the door when he put a hand on my shoulder.

"Can't you give us some idea?" he asked. "Just a general estimate? We've all got things to do…and of course we want to be here with him, but if he doesn't know we're in the room, and it might be drawn out…Well, you know what I mean."

I *did* know what he meant, and I moved away, causing his hand to fall from my shoulder.

"As I said, it's impossible to know."

This time I made it to the door and was turning the handle, when I looked over into the corner and caught the eye of Sue Mills. She understood the subtle nod of my head and started to follow me out of the room. That was when I noticed the woman standing beside her. She was in her mid-forties, stooped over with her hands clasped in front of her, and she was sobbing.

Out in the hallway, I turned to Sue and asked, "Tell me about those people in there." My face was still flushed, and I was angry.

"Well, you were talking with Jonas's son," she began. "It's really funny, though. We haven't seen him in months. In fact, we haven't seen any of them. Except…the woman standing in the corner with me. That's Eleanor Briggs, his granddaughter. She comes to visit almost every day. Has for years. They've been real close, and she's the only person he's ever asked about."

I was about to question her more about this family when she added, "I don't know if you're aware of it or not, but Mr. Griffin has a lot of money. Or at least that's what everyone says. You couldn't tell it by the way he acts, though. He's as down-to-earth as anybody. Always nice to the staff and never demanding. Not like his son," she added, nodding in the direction of cardiac. "A bunch of vultures, if you ask me. Everyone except Eleanor."

It took another three hours to get a bed ready upstairs. The ICU staff was coming down to get Mr. Griffin, and I was standing at the nurses' station with Lori Davidson.

"The family's already gone," she told me. "Got tired of waiting and took off. And Sue Mills went back to the nursing home. She asked that we call her if we hear anything."

I walked over to cardiac and quietly pushed the door open. Jonas was lying on the stretcher just as I had left him, breathing heavily with his eyes closed and his face expressionless.

But he wasn't alone. The ER has a way of separating the wheat from the chaff.

Eleanor Briggs was standing by the stretcher, quietly stroking the back of her grandfather's hand.

People are like stained-glass windows.
They sparkle and shine when the sun is out,
but when the darkness sets in,
their true beauty is revealed
only if there is a light from within.

ELISABETH KÜBLER-ROSS (1926–2004)

32

CORNERED

Have you ever done something you're really ashamed of? I mean something really bad?"

I had to be careful here. The question was coming from one of my sons, eleven years old at the time. I thought for a moment, struggling for the appropriate reply.

"Well, I think we've all done things we wished we hadn't," I answered. *Now to change the subject...*

"So tell me about one," came the quick response.

There would be no escape. This particular file cabinet was full to overflowing, but I reached into my memory for something not too embarrassing.

"Okay then," I said, and drew a breath as I began.

When I was a first-year medical student, our class—all one-hundred-twenty of us—had just started our second quarter and were beginning clinical pathology. We were two weeks into the course, when one of our instructors surprised us one morning and brought out several boxes of syringes, needles, alcohol swabs, and Band-Aids.

"All right," he told us. "Today you're going to learn to draw blood."

What? Thus far medical school had been pretty tame. Sure, we had dissected a human body in gross anatomy, but that hadn't been too bad, and we certainly hadn't experienced any personal pain. This drawing of blood, though—that was something different. That meant needles, and pain, and...well, maybe some lab techs were going to come in and demonstrate on real patients, or on themselves, or—

"You're going to practice on each other, so choose a partner and roll up your sleeves."

There was a collective sigh throughout the room, and we began pairing up with friends or someone close by. The trick was to pick an assistant who looked like they might be dexterous enough not to poke a bone or nerve.

I quickly latched onto one of my gross anatomy partners, someone who seemed to know what he was doing, and we began to collect the necessary equipment.

Wow! Those needles looked long…and sharp. While my friend and I pondered the execution of this task, some of the more aggressive students in our class had already begun prodding and sticking each other. There were cries of pain scattered around the room and then a commotion from somewhere near the door. One of the biggest guys in the class had passed out and was lying on the floor. Then another, and another. We were surrounded by pale and sweaty faces, wide eyes, and trembling hands. I looked at my partner, and we both glanced down at the waiting needles and syringes.

Without a word, our eyes met, we exchanged a nod, and we both reached down toward the tabletop. With steady hands and a complete lack of fear we each picked up a cotton ball and taped it in place in our elbows. Casually we strolled around the room, observing our fellow students as they struggled to find elusive veins amid grimaces and groans.

Then we looked at each other again, and down at our bandaged elbows. We walked back to our station, took off the cotton balls with a sigh, and I said, "Okay, who's first?"

He picked up a syringe and needle, then fished in his pocket for a coin. "Heads or tails?"

"Oh come on, Daddy," my son said, shaking his head. "What's so bad about that?

"Well…I mean…we were…" I stumbled.

"No, tell me something *really* bad," he insisted.

I knew I was going to have to tell him something, but what? And then I thought of Trudy, and what Jeff Ryan and I had done.

When I had first started working in the ER in Rock Hill, we had a night-shift nurse named Trudy. She was very capable and experienced. But at around three in the morning, she routinely became a little sleepy. That was true for all of us, but Trudy did something about it. If the ER was quiet, she would hunker down at the nurses' station with a Snickers bar and a blanket. After sitting down and eating her Snickers, she would lean over the desk, cover herself with her blanket, and fall asleep.

If only a few patients came in, Jeff Ryan, another night nurse, would usually handle it and let Trudy continue her nap. She was a sound sleeper and was sometimes hard to wake up.

We were having an unusually quiet night, with the ER empty of patients. The clock was approaching three a.m. Right on cue, Trudy went to the lounge, grabbed a Snickers, walked back to the nurses' station, and settled into her usual and customary position. Within minutes she was under her blanket, fast asleep.

Jeff and I were standing there, and I guess what they say is true—*idle hands are the devil's workshop.* We looked at each other and then down at the countertop. Trudy had left her old, worn stethoscope out in plain view, and it drew our attention. Without a word, I picked it up, made a snipping motion with my index and long fingers, and held out my hand. Jeff reached into his pocket, took out his scissors, and gave them to me.

I slipped the bell off the end of the scope, cut off about three-quarters of an inch of tubing, replaced the bell, and then carefully put the instrument back on the countertop. Jeff was smiling gleefully as we quickly made our way down the hall, with Trudy asleep under her blanket.

This went on for a couple of weeks whenever we had the chance. Some nights we were busy, and the Snickers and blanket never made it to the nurses' station. But there were enough opportunities to eventually shorten the scope to only four or five inches. Since we were doing it gradually, Trudy never seemed to notice—until late one Friday night.

One of our regulars had come in, having had way too much to drink. He could barely sit up in the triage chair while Trudy tried to get his vital signs. She was using her stethoscope to check his blood pressure. And it was all Jeff and I could do to not burst out laughing. She was leaning over, and the short length of the scope caused her to be right in his face. Suddenly he lurched to the side, turned his head, and kissed her on the mouth. Actually, it probably wasn't a kiss—more of a slobbery "hello."

We couldn't hold it any longer and laughed out loud. Trudy stood bolt upright, wiped her mouth, looked over at us, and then down at her stethoscope. The gig was up. I was on my feet quickly and pointed at Jeff. Then being quite brave, I turned and hurried down the hallway, leaving him to face Trudy's wrath.

"So were you ashamed of ruining her stethoscope or letting Jeff take the blame?" my boy asked.

"Neither," I told him. "We replaced her stethoscope. And it wasn't letting Jeff take the blame that bothered me. It was letting him get the credit for doing it. That was pretty clever, and has become something of an 'ER urban legend.' That's what I regret."

I leaned back in my chair and with finality slapped the tops of my thighs.

He just looked at me. Then he was looking *through* me. He must have known I was just scratching the surface.

Finally he shook his head and said, "Daddy, let me know when you're ready to come clean."

He stood up and headed for the door.

"Sure," I told him, sweating but relieved.

When he was out of sight, I muttered, "In about twenty years."

We own up to minor failings,
but only so as to convince others
that we have no major ones.

La Rochefoucauld (1613–1705)

33

Footsteps in the Sand

I'm not sure how we started talking about the beach, or who it was that brought it up. But it was clear that John Talford was more interested in talking about his trip a few months ago to Garden City than he was in listening to what I had to say about his chest X-ray and lab work. I needed to tell him his cancer had captured his entire right lung, and his anemia was getting dangerously worse.

"You know, Dr. Lesslie," he continued, "my wife and I used to have a place not too far from the pier—spent a lot of good times there."

"John," I began, trying to get a word in while he briefly paused. It didn't work, and he resumed his musing.

"She's been gone a couple of years now—died just a few days short of her ninetieth birthday. She really loved that place, you know."

He paused and glanced up at the clock on the wall. Then he turned back to me and sighed.

"I know you're busy, Dr. Lesslie, and I know what you're going to tell me about my X-ray. But I want to share something with you, something I think you need to hear. It will only take a moment." Without another word, he glanced down at the stool beside his stretcher. This time I didn't try to interrupt him. He had something important to say, and I wanted to hear it. I pulled the stool close and sat down.

There was something different about John tonight. Sure, his breathing was labored, worse than the past few times I had seen him. But that wasn't it. There was a peace about him, a warm glow in his eyes, and I felt a tangible comfort in his presence.

He interlocked his fingers and placed his hands on his chest, as if he were praying. Then without taking his eyes off mine, he began.

"I was down at the beach a few weeks ago with my family, and one morning I got up early and went for a walk. It was a little before sunrise, and I was the only one out there. I really wasn't paying much attention to what was going on around me, just walking along, thinking, enjoying the breeze in my face. After I while, I decided to turn around and head back to the house. That's when I started paying attention, and studied my footsteps in the sand. I was retracing them—and it was kind of strange, looking down at my own steps, the ones I had made only moments before. They were clear and sure. But as I got farther along, I noticed they started to get a little less distinct, and they started to fade away. I guess it was the wind and the sand. And the tide was starting to come in. And before I knew it, they were gone. Disappeared. There was no trace I had even passed this way."

He paused and continued to look into my eyes. His own were moist now, but still clear and strong and peaceful.

"I just stood there, Doc, and thought about that, and about…and then I looked up and the sun was pushing its way over the horizon. And the longer I watched, the stronger and brighter it got. And in a few minutes, I could feel its warmth on my face. And those footsteps…well, they didn't matter anymore."

We sat there a moment, studying each other.

Then John said, "Now, tell me about my X-ray."

I have fought the good fight,
I have finished the race,
I have kept the faith.

2 Timothy 4:7

34

Maybe This Time

L isa Matthews walked over to the nurses' station and just stood there, awkwardly waiting for something.

She was one of the hospital's lab techs and had just drawn some blood from the patient in room 3. I had his clipboard in my hand.

"Do you need this, Lisa?" I asked her, holding up the record.

"No," she answered, her voice quiet, almost timid. "I just wanted to thank you for trying to help my brother, Zeke. I know you guys did everything you could, and that…I know you really tried."

I looked up, but she was hurrying down the hallway before I could say anything.

"Poor Lisa," Amy said from the other side of the counter. "She's really taken this hard."

I sighed heavily and put the clipboard down on the counter, watching as the young tech disappeared around the corner.

"I wish there was something we could have done," I said. "That *somebody* could have done."

"Some people you just can't help," Amy spoke. "What's that they say about leadin' a horse to water?"

Virginia Granger walked up and said, "But you can't make 'em drink. What are you two talking about?"

"Zeke Matthews," Amy answered, spinning around in her chair and facing her head nurse. "Lisa's brother."

"I know Zeke," Virginia responded. "From way back."

She pulled a chair over beside Amy and sat down.

"Did I ever tell you about the time Zeke went over to one of the urgent-care centers in town to have a drug screen done?"

She looked at Amy and then over to me. We both shook our heads.

"Well, *that's* a story," she began. "One of my friends, Carla Patterson, worked in this particular center and was in charge of the drug screening. One day Zeke came in for a test—I think it must have been court-ordered or something. Apparently he wasn't too happy about being there, because my friend complained about his bad attitude, and she doesn't complain about anybody. Anyway, the first time he came in, he waited for a couple of hours and couldn't produce a specimen. Said he must be dehydrated or something. They sent him out and told him to come back the next day. Well, he did, but this time he gave them a cold specimen."

"A what?" Amy interrupted.

"A cold specimen," Virginia repeated. "One that couldn't have just been voided. It must have been less than body temperature and they wouldn't accept it. Apparently he went outside and came back a few minutes later and said he was ready to go again. This time the specimen was too hot, and they couldn't accept that one either."

"How did he do that?" Amy asked.

"I don't know," Virginia answered, shaking her head. "Maybe he had someone else's urine next to the heater in his car, to keep it warm. Only it got *too* warm."

"Now *that's* dedication," Amy remarked.

"It didn't stop there," Virginia continued. "Apparently the next step was to get a hair sample, usually from the back of a person's head, or if they're bald, from their arms or legs. It doesn't take much and only takes a minute. And it's hard to fake that.

"Anyway, they told Zeke what needed to happen and he got all huffy and left the clinic. But as I said, this was some kind of a legal drug screen and it had to be done. The next day he was at the front door when the clinic opened and said he was ready for his drug screen. But when they got him back to Carla's department, she said he was completely bald! The day before he'd had a full head of hair, but during the night he had completely shaved it off. Shaved his eyebrows too, and his arms and legs."

"What in the world did they do?" Amy asked, now sitting on the edge of her chair.

"Well, Carla said Zeke was just standing there smiling. That is, until she told him to raise his arms."

"What?" Amy exclaimed. "Do you mean she—"

"That's right, she clipped some hair from his armpits, and that was that."

"Did they bust him?" Amy asked. "Was it positive for something?"

"Cocaine and marijuana," I spoke up. "That's what Lisa told me the night he came in. That's what got him in trouble."

"Hmm," Virginia murmured. "You know, Carla said that what *really* got to her was his tattoo. You couldn't see it, because it was on the back of his head, and his hair usually covered it. But when he shaved, it was visible. She said it was an upside-down cross with *Zeke* written over it. That really bothered her."

"It would me too," Amy said, shaking her head. "I just wish someone could have gotten through to him."

"Well, a lot of people have tried," Virginia told her. "His family sure did, especially Lisa. He was in and out of rehab and in and out of jail, but she was always there for him. Always trying to find some other way to help him, some way to get him clean and keep him clean."

"What about his parents?" Amy asked. "I thought they kicked him out of the house. At least that's what Lisa told me."

"I think that's right," Virginia answered. "Carla Patterson knew his mother and that's how she knew the situation. She told me they had finally had enough. Hadn't completely given up on him, mind you, but after all, he was twenty-four years old. High-school dropout, no job, constantly stealing stuff from his folks. It was time for some tough love, and they finally made him leave."

"Still runnin' with the wrong crowd, I bet," Amy said. "It's hard to get straight when you do that."

"I had always *hoped* he would get straight, Amy," Virginia responded. "Maybe for some people it's just not possible. But you would hope…" her voice trailed off and she just sat there, all of us silent.

"I wonder if sometimes it's just too late," I mused. "If time just runs out."

"There's always hope," Virginia said firmly.

Amy looked up at her. "Always?"

Three weeks later, the ambulance entrance doors opened and two officers walked in. Between them, with hands cuffed and feet shackled, ambled a barefooted young man dressed in jeans and a dirty T-shirt.

I hadn't looked up until they had passed me and were headed down the hallway to minor trauma. Lori Davidson was waiting for them in the doorway, pointing to one of the stretchers. She had taken the call about the police bringing in a man with three stab wounds of his leg—something about an altercation following a drug deal.

One of the officers nodded at me, silently pointed at the man walking beside him, then frowned and shook his head. I had just enough time to see the scruffy back of the man's head and the tattoo—an upside-down cross with *Zeke* written over it.

Amy Connors had seen the same thing.

"Well, I'll be," she said. "Zeke Matthews. Maybe *this* is the time you can talk some sense into him."

I looked down at her and took a deep breath.

"Maybe."

Amy heard the doubt in my voice and said, "All we can do is keep tryin'."

When the world says "Give up,"
Hope whispers, "Try it one more time."

UNKNOWN

35

By the Book

This didn't make sense.

I took the X-ray off the view box and held it in front of the "hot light."

There must *be a fracture here somewhere. I just haven't found it yet.*

Once again I studied the X-rays of Mattie White's hip, turning it from side to side, looking for some irregularity.

The eighty-three-year-old had fallen earlier in the day. She lived alone, and was lucky. She had managed to pull down her phone and call 9-1-1. EMS had brought her in as "possible hip fracture" and she was now back in the ortho room.

Her right hip had been tender when I examined it, and she grimaced with pain when I tried to move the joint. Clinically she had a fracture, but I couldn't find one on the X-rays.

I put the films back on the stand below the view box and walked down the hallway. She was waiting patiently, rubbing her hands together as I walked in the room.

"Well, what did you find?" she asked me, putting her hands by her side and turning slightly to face me. Even this slight movement caused her pain, and she took a deep breath, bracing herself.

"Mattie," I said, sitting down on the rolling stool beside her stretcher. We were eye level, and she was able to settle back on the bed and find a more comfortable position. "I can't see a fracture on your X-ray, but you have one. And I know it's there."

She studied my face for a moment then said, "Dr. Lesslie, what does that mean? What are we to do now?"

She was smiling at me patiently, like a grandmother might do.

"Well, the next step will be to get an MRI of that hip," I explained. "It's much more sensitive than a plain X-ray and will show us that fracture."

"Good," she said firmly. "Let's get that done."

"Well, there's a problem," I told her. "It's eight o'clock at night and the hospital won't do an MRI this time of day. We'll have to wait until tomorrow."

Her shoulders sank a little and she looked down at her hands.

"What are we to do until then?" she asked, looking up once more.

I had already thought about this question and considered our options. The ER was crowded—every bed full—so keeping her down here wouldn't be possible. Besides, the beds in ortho weren't very comfortable and she would have a miserable night. And I couldn't send her home. Mattie had a broken hip—I just knew it. The MRI would be positive and she would be in the OR tomorrow to have it fixed. Besides, she lived alone and had no family in town. She was on her own.

The last possibility was to get the orthopedist on call to put her in the hospital overnight and get the scan in the morning. I didn't have hard evidence of a fractured hip, but most of the ortho docs were reasonable and would probably do that for me.

I told her of this last option and she nodded and thanked me.

"Let me make a phone call and I'll be back in a few minutes."

I could hear the EMS radio squawking as I approached the nurses' station. There were three ambulances out on calls. It was going to be a long night.

"Susie, would you get ortho on the phone?" I asked our secretary.

Fifteen minutes later she called over to me. "Dr. Lesslie, I've got Dr. Johnson."

I walked over and she handed me the receiver.

"Steve, this is Robert."

"What is it?" came the curt response. Steve Johnson wasn't our favorite orthopedist, for a number of reasons. He was quick to second-guess us over the phone, slow to come in to see his patients, and frequently rude to them when he did.

Susie had already heard the tone of his voice and was looking up at me, shaking her head. I rolled my eyes.

"I've got an eighty-three-year-old lady here with a fractured hip. No other medical problems and she's stable, but she'll have to come in."

I held my breath, hoping for a simple and positive response.

"Where is the fracture?" he asked. "What part of the hip?"

I hesitated a moment and then explained the X-ray findings.

"She's *got* a fracture," I said. "But it's going to take an MRI to find it."

"Why are you calling *me?*" he asked, his voice with more of an edge now. "If she doesn't have a fracture, I don't need to be admitting her to the hospital."

I repeated my findings and explained her personal situation.

"She can't walk, has no one at home to take care of her, and needs to be in the hospital." I was checking myself, trying not to let my voice betray my rising impatience and anger.

"You might be right about being in the hospital, Robert," he responded. "But I'm not going to admit her. It's not an orthopedic problem. Maybe *you* should admit her."

My face was steaming, and I took a deep breath. He knew the doctors in the ER didn't admit patients to the hospital. With great difficulty I didn't take the bait.

"Steve, this woman needs your help and—"

"Listen," he interrupted. "When Medicare audits her record, who do you think is going to be in trouble? It won't be you, will it? It will be me. And that's just not going to happen."

"You won't even have to come see her tonight," I found myself pleading. "I'll write the orders and—"

Click.

I held the phone in front of me and stared at it, wanting desperately to smash it against something.

"Is he going to put her in?" Susie asked quietly.

"Nope."

I headed down the hallway to Mattie, wondering what to try next.

"What's the matter?" she asked, looking over at me as I entered the room.

"Nothing," I lied. "We'll need to—"

"What's the matter, Dr. Lesslie?" she persisted. "You're troubled about something."

I wasn't going to bother her with my conversation with Steve Johnson, or with the bind he had put us in. But the peaceful look in her eyes and the smile on her face calmed my anger. I told her what had just transpired.

"Maybe he's had a bad day," she said patiently. "Or maybe he doesn't feel well."

"No," I said flatly. "I'm afraid that's just the way he is."

"Hmm," she murmured, placing a hand to her chin. "Sometimes we need to overlook how people act and how they treat us. We need to have some patience, even though it can be very difficult. And Dr. Lesslie, you just never know when you'll need someone to overlook *your* actions and be patient with *you*."

Mattie was smiling up at me, and of course she was right. But this was a *righteous* impatience, a *righteous* anger, and it felt good.

"But Mattie, this man is really difficult to deal with. He could help us here, but he's too headstrong, too self-centered. He's determined to play by the book, no matter who gets hurt."

She nodded at me, and her smile still shone warmly.

"I suppose it depends on *which* Book we're playing by, doesn't it, Dr. Lesslie? And that's *your* choice to make, not his."

I looked down at Mattie and studied her timeworn face, each line and wrinkle tracing years of wisdom. Our eyes met and I knew she was studying me as well. But there was no judgment there, only concern and a desire for me to release my destructive emotion.

A deep sigh escaped my lips.

"Now, Dr. Lesslie," she continued, "what are we going to do?"

My anger was gone, and I was thinking clearly again.

"I'm going to call one of my cardiology friends and ask him for a favor. We'll have him put you in the hospital, get the MRI in the morning, and go from there."

"That sounds fine," Mattie said, nestling her head back in the small pillow. She closed her eyes, smiled, and repeated, "That sounds fine."

Mattie's MRI the next morning demonstrated a fracture of her hip, and by midafternoon she was in the OR, having it repaired.

Steve Johnson was the orthopedist present, and he didn't bother to apologize or admit he had been wrong. But it no longer mattered. Mattie and I were playing by a different Book.

Teach me Thy patience; still with Thee
In closer, dearer company,
In work that keeps faith sweet and strong,
In trust that triumphs over wrong.

From the hymn "O Master, Let Me Walk with Thee"
by Washington Gladden (1836–1918)

36

SAY WHAT?

It was the middle of the night, and we had only one patient in the entire ER. The triage nurse had just taken a twenty-three-year-old man to room 4. After pulling the curtain closed, she walked over to the nurses' station, shaking her head.

Amy Connors was the secretary on duty. She took the clipboard from the nurse.

"Well, duh!" she smirked, logging in the patient and pushing the chart over to me.

I glanced down at the chief complaint. "Smoking cocaine. Feels funny." His vital signs were completely normal.

"He's fine," the nurse told me. "Said he was smokin' with some friends and got a little light-headed and dizzy. Feels okay now. Just wants to be sure everything is alright."

"Sounds like one for 'the list,'" Amy chuckled. As I walked over to room 4, she reached into one of the drawers and took out a worn black-leather notebook.

Our young patient turned out to be fine. He had no medical problems from his cocaine abuse, though I took the opportunity to educate him about the potential of life-threatening complications associated with its use. He might have been listening.

As he left through the triage entrance I slumped into a chair next to Amy. Jeff Ryan was sitting next to me, thumbing through an ancient edition of *People* magazine.

"Well, he makes the list," Amy said. "But he's not an 'all-star.'"

She had opened the black notebook and was adding his complaint to a long list of noteworthy entries.

"Let me take a look at that when you're finished," I remarked. It had been a while since I had perused its pages and was curious about any recent additions.

"Now is this stuff for real?" Jeff asked, tossing his magazine to the countertop.

"Of course it is!" Amy answered, handing me the book. "It's what the triage nurse writes down when a patient tells them why they're in the ER—word for word. Just like that guy with the cocaine."

I had already read a few and was laughing out loud.

"Come on, Doc, read 'em to us," Jeff said, rolling his chair a little closer. "Don't hog it."

"Okay, okay," I said, flipping the pages back to the beginning. They were all handwritten, logged in by various people. The date of the first entry was more than 15 years earlier.

"Here we go," I told them, leaning back in my chair and holding the notebook with both hands.

- *One of my earrings is missing. I had it on when I went to bed and think I must have swallowed it.*
- *My hair is falling out (19 yr old female).*
- *My hair isn't growing (54 yr old female, mother of the above).*
- *My tongue came out last night.*
- *I fell two hours ago and I think I got killed.*
- *I swallowed a spoon.*
- *I'm missing a tooth and think I swallowed it.*
- *I've got a headache in my stomach.*
- *I blacked out and can't remember yesterday.*
- *My dog has the mange and now I'm itching.*
- *I can't tell a woman my problem (22 yr old man).*
- *I'm hearing voices and I don't like the music.*
- *I'm weak and dizzy and can't see straight.*
- *(From an interpreter) My friend here had his tongue bitten off by his girlfriend.*

"I remember that guy!" Jeff interrupted. "That was about three years ago and he came in about this time of night. Had a big chunk missing from the tip. Boy, was he mad."

"What about the guy who swallowed his grandfather's watch?" Amy asked. "I'm sure he made the list."

"Let's see," I said, flipping over a few pages. "That would be in the 'swallowed stuff' section."

We had several pages of items purportedly swallowed by our patients:

* *an unopened safety pin*
* *an opened safety pin*
* *a straight pin*
* *a ballpoint pen*
* *assorted coins (including a silver dollar and a Russian ruble)*
* *keys*
* *a sharpened pencil*
* *a small harmonica*
* *a soft drink cap*
* *assorted pieces of glass*
* *a whistle*
* *a diamond ring*
* *a cubic zirconia ring*
* *various chess pieces*
* *checkers*
* *Monopoly game board pieces*
* *thumbtacks*
* *pushpins*
* *paperclips*
* *dice*
* *a razor blade*
* *a small closed pocketknife*
* *assorted nuts and bolts*
* *marbles*
* *fishing sinkers*
* *fishing hooks*
* *fish bones*
* *chicken bones*
* *pork-chop bones*
* *a ham bone*
* *toy soldiers*
* *toy animals*
* *Legos*
* *Lincoln logs*
* *fuses*
* *a variety of batteries*
* *broken thermometers*
* *multiple teeth*
* *dentures*
* *buttons*
* *washers (not Maytag)*

And then, there it was—*my grandfather's watch.*

"See!" Amy exclaimed. "I remember that guy. I wonder if he ever got it back."

I lowered the notebook and looked over at her. "Well, Amy, time passes."

"Yeah," she nodded absently. Then suddenly she looked over at me with squinted eyes and scrunched face. "Oooo…"

"Find the all-star list," Jeff interjected. "I bet there's some good stuff there."

I held up the notebook again and turned to the last few pages. There, on a much thumbed and worn sheet was written: "ER All-Stars." There were only a dozen or so entries here, so this had to be a very select group.

I noticed that something had been copied and taped to the opposite page. It was part of the hospital's patient information sheet. A section of it was circled in red, and I glanced over it.

When I laughed aloud, Amy said, "Come on, what is it?"

"It's the family history part of the record, where the patient is asked about their parents' state of health and, if they're deceased, the cause of death. This particular patient wrote *Mississippi* and *heart attack*."

They both chuckled as I looked back at the "All-Star" page and scanned down to the bottom. I recognized my own handwriting, read the first line, and closed the book.

"What's the matter?" Jeff asked.

"Nothing. I just know the story and it's still one of the best ever."

EMS had brought twenty-year-old John Doe into the department and deposited him in room 5.

"Looks like too much cheap wine," the paramedics told me. "No evidence of any trauma, just hard to wake up. His friends called it in and then took off."

As I was examining John and being nearly overcome by alcohol fumes, I noticed the "medical alert" tag hanging around his neck. The flip side read "Diabetic."

"Let's get a blood sugar, stat," I told the nurse. "And we need to get an IV started."

While we continued to work on him, I would call out his name, trying to get whatever information I could.

"John, tell me about your diabetes!" I asked, close to his ear and loud.

His eyes opened for a moment and rolled lazily in my direction. He smiled and closed them again.

"John, are you using insulin?"

Alcohol or not, he could have overdosed on his medication and dangerously lowered his blood sugar.

This time his head jerked a little and he looked straight at me.

"Insulin?" he mumbled. "I'm not on insulin."

"Good—then tell me what you take for your diabetes."

His brow furrowed and he stuck out his lower lip. Finally he said, "Diabetes? I don't have diabetes."

I reached down and grabbed his medical alert tag.

"But this says you're a diabetic!" I told him.

"No, not a diabetic," he answered, smiling up at me. "I have seizures, and when I went to the drugstore, they didn't have the 'Epilepsy' tag, so I got this instead."

His head plopped back onto the bed and he closed his eyes.

"Say what?" Jeff exclaimed, laughing.

"That's what I thought, Jeff. *Say what?*"

A cheerful heart is good medicine,
but a downcast spirit dries up the bones.

PROVERBS 17:22

37

Under His Wings

L ori hurriedly pushed the wheelchair through the triage entrance and past the nurses' station. Without saying a word, she let me know the man in the chair was in trouble. The look in her eye and the nod of her head were all I needed. I put the chart I was holding down on the desk and followed her into room 5.

It was Greg Layton. He was a fifty-two-year-old farmer and tough as nails. Or at least he *had* been when I first met him in the ER seven months ago.

He had come in then with a cough that wouldn't go away. But that wouldn't have been enough to bring him to the hospital that morning. It was the blood he had coughed up that had him troubled.

"Yeah, Doc, I feel okay, but that sorta got me worried."

I had sat down on the stool beside his stretcher and listened. He quickly changed the subject, and the worried look on his face soon faded as he started telling me about himself.

He was farming the same land his family had for over a hundred years, and unlike a lot of farmers in the area, he was making a living.

"It's a lot of hard work," he told me. "But I can't imagine doin' anything else. I guess it's in my blood."

This was a good man, and underneath the sun-leathered exterior was a kindness and gentleness that radiated from his eyes. Yet those same eyes betrayed his fear as he grew silent and shifted nervously on the stretcher.

"I guess you need to know I'm a smoker," he said quietly. "Started when I was thirteen. Should have listened to my ma, but it was…you know, it was the thing to do back then. And once I got started, I couldn't stop. Goin' to now, though. Smoked my last one this mornin'."

He did stop smoking, but it was too late. His lung cancer was aggressive and had already occupied almost a third of his chest, pushing on his airways and his blood vessels. When I had looked at his chest X-ray, I was surprised that he wasn't having more symptoms and trouble from this disease that was going to take his life.

The time he had left would be measured in weeks and months, not years, and we talked about that and about his options.

The cancer specialists were even blunter.

"Three months, maybe four, if you're lucky," they had told him.

"Lucky?" he had responded. "Somehow I don't feel so lucky."

But he was tough as nails and had stayed on his tractor for as long as he could. The months went by, the few that remained, and he had somehow stayed out of the ER. I had thought about him every once in a while and wondered how he was doing, or even if he was still alive. Then suddenly here he was before me, again in the ER.

"Blood pressure is low," Lori told me as we helped Greg up onto the stretcher. "And he's got a temp of 102."

Greg looked awful, but somehow managed a smile as Lori and I easily lifted his wasting frame to the bed. He moaned quietly as we tried to make him as comfortable as we could.

He was gasping for breath and not moving much air. While I quickly listened to his chest, Lori connected the nasal prongs to the oxygen line and carefully placed it around his head and into his nose.

"Thanks," he whispered, looking up at her.

Once again, I was struck by the passage of time and the changes it brings. It had only been a few months since I had first seen this man. Then, though he was harboring a fatal cancer, he had been strong and fit and full of life. I hadn't seen him since, and the man lying before me could easily have been someone else. He could barely raise his arms from his side, and his sallow skin hung loosely on his ravaged body.

Yet his eyes were the same. There was that unmistakable kindness and… something else. There was a peace there, a calmness that could come from no other place than his heart.

He glanced up at Lori and saw the troubled look on her face.

"Ma'am, don't worry," he tried to reassure her. "I'll be okay."

And then he looked over at me. "And don't you worry either, Doc. Just do what you can."

His words were labored and came between painful and difficult gasps.

"Try to relax," I told him, putting my hand on his bony shoulder. "Let the oxygen help."

He nodded, tired from the effort of these few words. Then with a sudden movement that surprised Lori and me, he reached up for his shirt pocket and fumbled around for something. When he finally took his hand away, he stretched it out to me, revealing a crumpled and tattered piece of paper.

"Here," he murmured, now barely audible. "This is for you. Both of you."

Less than an hour later he was on his way to the ICU, his wife walking silently by the side of his stretcher. He was still struggling for the few breaths that remained to him.

Somehow, as he had passed the nurses' station, he had managed to tell us, "I'll be okay."

Lori and I watched as they disappeared around the corner at the back of the department.

"What was on that piece of paper he gave you?" she asked me.

I reached into my coat pocket and took it out, carefully unfolding it.

He had scribbled "Psalm 91:4-6" on it, and I looked down at Amy Connors, our unit secretary.

"Amy, would you hand me our Bible?"

She opened one of the drawers beside her and took out a worn and tattered black-leather book.

"Here," she said, sliding it across the counter to me.

I found Greg's passage and Lori and I silently read it.

> He will cover you with his feathers,
> and under his wings you will find refuge;
> his faithfulness will be your shield and rampart.
> You will not fear the terror of night,
> nor the arrow that flies by day,
> nor the pestilence that stalks in the darkness,
> nor the plague that destroys at midday.
> Psalm 91:4-6

Greg Layton was going to be okay.

38

MANDY

I diagnosed Mandy Jenkins with diabetes when she was four years old. Actually, it was Lori Davidson who had made the diagnosis. Lori was in triage when Mandy's mother brought her to the ER. It was late at night, and the little girl had a fever and cough. As Lori checked her temperature, she noticed Mandy's labored breathing and sunken eyes. According to her mother, she didn't have any medical problems and didn't take any medication. Lori's antenna was up.

"How long has this been going on?" she asked Ms. Jenkins. "How long has Mandy been sick?"

It turned out she had started losing weight a few weeks earlier and was becoming more and more listless. Then yesterday the fever and cough had started.

Lori's nephew had developed diabetes at about the same age, and it had declared itself in the same way: subtle, gradual changes—and then a rapid worsening.

"I'm going to check a blood sugar before we get her back to a bed," Lori explained, deftly pricking the tip of one of Mandy's fingers. She didn't flinch, another bothersome sign.

The monitor flashed the answer: 485. Her blood sugar was sky-high and she was in trouble.

After a couple of hours, Mandy was stabilized and on her way upstairs. She remained in the hospital for a few days until her newly uncovered disease was under control.

When we saw her two years later, it was for a broken wrist. She had been trying out for the cheerleading squad of one of the teams in the town's midget football league. An awkwardly landed tumble had bent her arm under her, resulting in a greenstick fracture of her left wrist. Nothing serious, and it would heal quickly.

As Lori and I were applying a splint to her injured arm, Mandy proudly showed us her new insulin pump.

"We got it two weeks ago," her mother explained. "And it works great. It's made a big difference with her blood sugars."

"That's right," Mandy agreed. Then pointing down to the device, "And it's got knobs to turn up and down. See?"

She was about to demonstrate how this was done when her mother quickly reached out and gently grabbed her hand.

"No, we don't need to do that," she told her daughter. "I'm sure they know how it works."

I was glad to see they were using the pump. It meant they had a good handle on her management, and it would mean better control of her diabetes and hopefully fewer complications down the road.

Noticing her outfit I asked, "When did you get interested in cheerleading?"

Mandy looked down and smoothed her pleated and now rumpled skirt with her good hand.

"Last year," her mother answered. "We want to keep her as active as we can and as normal as we can. And this is something she's always been interested in."

The little girl looked up at us and smiled. Her light-blue eyes were sparkling, setting off her curly blonde hair. She was a beautiful child and you couldn't help staring at her.

"Well, I think she's going to be a star," I said. "As soon as she learns how to tumble without breaking stuff."

Mandy giggled, cut her eyes away, and shrugged her shoulders.

"Trouble," I whispered to her mother. She smiled and nodded.

Over the next few years we learned that Mandy Jenkins had developed into quite an accomplished cheerleader. Her squad had won several area competitions and even placed second in one of the state contests. She also had become a soccer star, playing on the varsity team while still in the seventh grade. She wasn't letting her diabetes hold her back.

Then something changed.

EMS 2 had called it in.

"We've got a sixteen-year-old female—unresponsive—no blood pressure."

When the paramedics came through the ambulance entrance Lori immediately directed them to the cardiac room.

"It's Mandy Jenkins!" she called over to me.

I was standing at the nurses' station and immediately turned and looked down at the stretcher.

"What's her blood sugar?" I asked, reaching down and checking Mandy's pulse. Rapid and barely detectable, but it was there.

"Too high to read," one of the paramedics answered. "We got a line started and came in as fast as we could."

She was breathing, but with rapid, shallow gasps. And she didn't respond to my loudly calling her name.

We got her into cardiac and quickly swarmed around her.

Lori started another IV while a technician from the lab drew blood. Radiology was in the room, waiting to shoot a chest X-ray, and after I secured her airway, I looked around for someone who could give us some information.

"Is her mother here?" I asked one of the paramedics, now standing in the doorway.

"No, she was at home by herself," he answered. "The call came in from someone who said he was a friend, but they were gone when we got to the house."

This didn't make sense. Her insulin pump was in place on her side, so why would her blood sugar be so high?

"Over 800," the lab tech called out, handing me Mandy's lab slip. "The blood sugar is over 800!"

That explained what was going on—she was probably dangerously acidotic and her electrolytes were probably all out of whack. *But why?*

I looked down at her labs and there was the blood sugar in bold numbers—**811**. I was about to toss the piece of paper to the countertop when I saw it, buried in the other abnormal numbers. Her creatinine was 5.5! She was in kidney failure. But that sort of thing didn't happen overnight.

I glanced over at Lori. She was looking down at Mandy's hands and elbows, checking for any needle marks. We had to consider anything and everything here, and drug use was a possibility.

Lori looked up at me and shook her head. Her skin was clear.

That was good, but yet...

The door of the room burst open and Mandy's mother stood there, frantically taking in the confusing but controlled chaos. When she saw her daughter, she hurried over to the stretcher and grabbed her hand.

"What's happened?" she screamed. "Is she going to be all right?"

She was looking up at me now, with eyes wide and face flushed.

I told her what we knew and what we were doing.

"She's starting to respond a little," I told her. "But she's very sick and will need to be in the ICU until she's out of the woods."

Ms. Jenkins looked down at her daughter again and began shaking her head.

"I should have listened to her," she whispered.

Lori's head jerked around and she stared at the woman.

"You should have listened to what?" I asked, stepping closer.

"I really didn't think she would...or that this might happen..." she muttered to herself.

"You should have listened to what?" I repeated, a little louder this time.

She looked up at me and said, "You know Mandy's always been into cheerleading and things like that. She's the class president and was runner-up to the homecoming queen. And she's always been worried about her weight." She paused and sighed, shaking her head again. "Her father and I have tried to convince her she's a perfect size, but she...she was always weighing herself and always watching everything she ate."

"You should have listened to what?" I interrupted, the edge in my voice caused Lori to look over at me.

Speaking more quickly now, Mandy's mother continued. "A couple of weeks ago, she just happened to mention that she had learned something new. That if she cut back on her insulin, she would lose weight. It really didn't register...but do you think that could have anything to do with this?"

Lori reached down and pulled the sheet away from Mandy's side, exposing the insulin pump. She turned it over in her hand and held it up so I could see the controls.

It had been turned off.

Do not wish to be anything but what you are,
and try to be that perfectly.

St. Francis de Sales (1567–1622)

39

No Warranties

The door to triage opened and Allen Jeffers came into the department—in a wheelchair.

He seemed none too happy as he was rolled by the nurses' station and down the hallway to the ortho room. Lori Davidson handed me his chart on the way back out to triage.

"Hope you can cheer this one up," she said, shaking her head. "He's not in a very good mood."

I glanced down at his record.

48 yr old male—injured heel

"He looks familiar," I said to her, trying to place him.

"He's on the city council," Lori answered. "You might have seen him on TV," she added, then smiled and headed back out to triage.

"And again, good luck!" she tossed over her shoulder.

Hmm…Not very many people *are* in a good mood when they come to the ER, so what was up with this guy? Looked like he had gotten Lori's attention.

I walked down the hallway and into ortho. Jeffers was still in his wheelchair, leaning forward and rubbing his left ankle. He looked up as I entered. "Listen, Doc, I need an MRI. And then you can call Dr. Jackson, my orthopedist."

"Well, let's take a look—"

"No, just get the MRI!" he interrupted. "I know it's broken. I heard it snap while I was running. Man, this just isn't fair!"

Allen Jeffers was a trim, middle-aged man, dressed in running shoes and a sleek, dark-blue running suit.

"Well, if it's broken, we'll need to get an X-ray first and—"

"No, that's just a waste of time," he insisted, slapping his knees and looking up at me.

I see what Lori was talking about.

The next five minutes were spent in negotiation, with me explaining what the process *needed* to be, and Allen Jeffers insisting what it *would* be. Finally, he allowed me to examine his injured limb, and I was immediately able to tell him his problem.

"I don't think you have a fracture. You've torn your Achilles tendon. That was the snapping sound you heard, and the sudden pain."

"My Achilles..." he stammered. "How can you..."

I explained the injury to him, compared the movement of his left foot with his right foot, and finally convinced him of what was going on.

"You *will* need to see Dr. Jackson," I told him. "And you'll need an operation to repair it."

"An operation?" he exclaimed. "Exactly what are we talking about here? And how much time out of work? And—"

"Let's not get ahead of ourselves," I tried to calm him. But the fact remained, this was a bad injury, and he was in for a long haul. It would be months before he would be able to run again.

"I don't understand it," he scowled. "Are you sure?"

He was feeling the back of his heel and trying to raise his foot. It wouldn't move.

He shook his head and grumbled, "This shouldn't be happening to me. I've always taken care of my body. I exercise every day and take a ton of vitamins. I don't smoke, never have. I've always...and now...now this! Weeks on crutches! No running for...how long did you say? Oh, it doesn't matter. This shouldn't be happening. It's just not fair."

I left him fuming in his wheelchair and walked back to the nurses' station.

"Amy, would you get Dr. Jackson on the phone? And call around to the OR supervisor."

Not long after that, Lori wheeled another patient into the department. "Hello, Dr. Lesslie."

I turned around and looked down at Curtis Bartram.

Curtis was in his late seventies but looked much younger. His four decades of working with the city, most of them out of doors, had kept him active and in good shape. Though retired now, he was still fit and trim.

So why was he in a wheelchair?

"Hey, Curtis," I responded, grabbing his hand. "What brings you to the ER today?"

"Just not feelin' well, Doc," he said. "Got up from my chair a little while ago and got real light-headed. Almost passed out."

I looked closer at him, for the first time noticing the color of his face. I reached out and gently pulled down his right lower eyelid. Pale. Almost white. He was anemic, and losing blood.

"What's his—"

"90 over 60," the triage nurse interrupted. "And his pulse is 110."

"Where are you headed?" I asked her.

"Room 4," she told me as she pushed off in that direction.

"I'll be right there," I told Curtis. Then turning to Amy Connors I said, "We need lab down here stat. And try to get his old records."

She was already on the phone as I finished up the chart in front of me and tossed it into the discharge basket.

We spent the next couple of hours getting Curtis stabilized and trying to determine the source of his blood loss. He wasn't having any pain and continued to insist that he felt fine—except for that light-headed episode earlier.

"Here's his old record," Amy told me, sliding the folder across the counter. "It's all they could find."

The file was thin, much thinner than I would have thought. I remembered seeing him in the ER a few years earlier with acute appendicitis, and those records were there. But that was all. At seventy-eight years of age you would think he would have been in the hospital more than just that one time.

He had walked into the ER that afternoon, saying that he had some belly pain and a little fever. "Nothing serious," he had told us. When I examined his right lower abdomen, however, he almost jumped off the table. Yet he didn't complain, and apologized for "being so tender." Two hours later his surgeon informed me that Curtis's appendix had been "red hot" and close to bursting. He had been lucky, and was back home in two days.

I flipped through the chart, looking for his weight on that visit: 178 lbs. And now, four years later, he weighed 162. That surprised me. And it was a problem.

His labs returned and they were a problem as well. He was dangerously anemic, with a hemoglobin of only 6. He would need a transfusion, and we needed to find out where he was bleeding.

I walked back into his room and sat down beside his stretcher.

"Curtis, you've lost some weight since you were last here."

He nodded and smiled at me. "I noticed my pants were getting a little loose, but I've been trying to eat, and I haven't been on a diet or anything."

I looked into his eyes and saw something I hadn't noticed before. He wasn't telling me something, maybe because he didn't think it was important. Or maybe he was afraid.

"Curtis, has there been anything different going on recently? Anything unusual?"

He sighed and began rubbing his hands together.

"The last couple of weeks…" He hesitated a moment, then finally took a deep breath. "The last couple of weeks or so, I've had trouble swallowing. The first time it was some roast beef I had cooked. But then it was almost anything I tried to eat of any size. And now, I can get down applesauce, but that's about all."

He was looking at me intently and must have seen me tense.

"What's the matter?" he asked quietly. "What are you thinking?"

He needed to know, and I told him.

"We're going to need a CT scan of your chest, Curtis. With your weight loss and bleeding, and with your difficulty swallowing, I'm concerned there might be something going on with your esophagus."

"Cancer?" he asked plainly, his expression unchanged.

"That would be the worst."

And it *was* the worst. His CT scan showed a mass in the middle of his chest, almost completely closing his esophagus. It was a wonder he had been able to get anything down.

After a week in the hospital and a battery of tests and procedures, his physicians gave him their opinion. And it wasn't anything anyone would want to hear. The cancer was inoperable, and they had little to offer other than radiation treatments to buy some time—and after that, inevitably, only pain medicine. And it wasn't going to be very long.

I knew all of this when he came through the ER on his way home. He was in a wheelchair again, and wanted to speak with me before he left the hospital.

"I was hoping you were on duty today, Dr. Lesslie," he told me, signaling the aide to stop at the nurses' station. "I wanted to thank you for all your help."

I searched his eyes again, looking for the fear and uncertainty I had seen there when he first came in. Instead there was a peaceful clarity and a reassuring calmness. And I realized *he* was reassuring *me*. He smiled and said, "I'm going to be alright. I've almost had my fourscore years and they've been good ones. The Lord has blessed me far more than I've deserved. And this body…" He paused and slapped the tops of his thighs. "This body was bound to give out on me one day. I've always known that. And that day has come."

He continued to look up at me, but I didn't know what to say. I just nodded.

"I'll be alright."

We shook hands one last time, and his nurse wheeled him out through the ambulance entrance. The doors closed behind them, and I never saw Curtis Bartram again.

But I know he's alright.

My flesh and my heart may fail,
but God is the strength of my heart
and my portion forever.

PSALM 73:26

40

The Days Before Penicillin

3 *:00 a.m.* "Wow, that was pretty neat!"
We were all sitting behind the desk at the nurses' station, having emptied the department of our last patient, a seven-year-old. He had come in with nausea, vomiting, and a little fever. Nothing specific. But he had tenderness in the right lower quadrant of his abdomen, which pointed to his appendix. He was being taken to the operating room now to have it removed.

"He didn't look that sick when he came in," John added. He was a senior pre-med student at Clemson, home for the Christmas holidays and spending some time with us in the ER.

Amy Connors was the unit secretary tonight, and she rolled back in her chair and looked over at the young man.

"You gotta stay on your toes around here," she told him solemnly, then winked in my direction. "You just never know."

"But what would have happened if we...if you had missed it, Dr. Lesslie? Would his appendix have ruptured? Doesn't that happen?"

I explained to John the pathology of appendicitis, how it happens, and what we know of its natural course.

He was sitting on the edge of his chair, with his hands on his knees. Occasionally he would purse his lips and nod his head. I felt like Aristotle.

"He's going to be okay, right?" he asked me. "But what would have happened, say, a hundred years ago? Or two hundred years ago? Would he just die? What could have been done before we knew how to operate on people?"

"That's a good question," I answered. "I would think most people with appendicitis didn't do so well. Someone might have put a poultice or something on their belly and hoped for the best. But the body has a way of dealing with a lot of things, and the appendix or even an abscess might have been walled off and the patient might have survived. Not very good chances, though, I would imagine."

"And even then, what about diabetes?" Jeff Ryan, our overnight nurse joined in. "Or heart disease? Or even pneumonia? Back in the day before antibiotics."

"That's right!" John exclaimed. "What did we ever do before penicillin and things like that?" He was bouncing on his toes now and looking around at each of us.

"Got sick and died," Amy muttered quietly.

"Hold it right there!" I announced, jumping up from my chair. Then looking down at the pre-med student, "I've got something you might be interested in. I'll be right back."

The medical journal was lying on a corner of the desk in our office and I thumbed through its pages, looking for the article I had come across a few days ago. Dealing with some obscure medical history, it had struck me as being interesting. This should be right up John's alley.

I walked back to the nurses' station, took my seat, and held up the journal for all to see.

"I'm going to read something to you, and it may shed a little light on some of your questions, John. If nothing else, it should make you appreciate where we are in medicine and how far we've come."

Jeff leaned back in his chair and folded his hands behind his head. "No Florence Nightingale stuff, is it?" he asked. "Or Clara Barton?"

"No, much older than that," I told him. "And a lot more interesting."

"Well, get started," Amy said, frowning at me. "You never know when we're gonna get busy again."

"Okay, okay," I said, flipping to the article. "But first, let me give you a little background. You may or may not be aware—I certainly wasn't—that William Shakespeare's son-in-law was a physician. A man named John Hall."

"When would that have been?" Jeff interrupted. "1500s or 1600s?"

"I think that was about right," I answered. "Certainly before Star Wars and Twinkies."

"Twinkies?" John asked, confusion in his voice. "What the—"

"Never mind," Amy chided him. "Go ahead, Dr. Lesslie. Let's hear what you got."

I settled into my chair and began.

"All right, it seems that this John Hall fellow was very precise about recording his treatments and outcomes. In fact, he kept an extensive

journal of his patients and their diseases. Some of them are recorded here."
I tapped the journal in my lap. "Here's the first one."

I opened the magazine, adjusted my glasses, and began.

"*Mrs. Smith of Stratford upon Avon, aged 54, being miserably afflicted
with a hot distillation in her eyes* [pink eye], *so that she could not open them
in the morning, was cured thus. First there was administered for four nights
together when she went to bed, three ounces of goat's milk and coal tar, made
into pills. These gave five or six bowel movements without pain the following
day. In the interim, to the eyes were applied the following: a spoonful of the
juice of houseleek* [an herb] *and white wine, mixed together. This was dropt
into the eyes, one drop each, laying upon them all night a double linen rag wet
with the same. By this she was cured.*"

"That doesn't sound so bad," Amy opined. "All except the coal tar part."

"I'll remind you of that next time you get conjunctivitis," Jeff said. "Go
ahead, Doc—what's next?"

I turned the page, found my marked paragraph, and began reading.

"*A Mr. Hudson, a poor man, labored of a swimming in the head* [vertigo].
I caused a quart of blood to be taken from the cephalica [a vein in the back
of the head], *and purged him with coal tar, rhubarb, vinegar, oak tree ashes,
and various herbs. This gave nine stools. Lastly, he took a half pound of dried
peacock dung infused in white wine and strained.*"

"He drank that stuff?" Amy exploded.

"Shhh!" Jeff chastised her. "Go ahead, Doc."

"Yes, Amy. He drank it," I told her.

"*And this he continued from New Moon to Full Moon, and was cured.*"

"I bet he told the doctor he was cured whether he was or not," Jeff said,
shaking his head. "What else you got?"

"One more," I told him, flipping the page.

"*Rogers of Stratford, aged 17, did labour of vomiting, jaundice, stopping
of the courses* [he couldn't void] *and bleeding at the nose. He received the following: half a spoonful of syrup of violets, four ounces of coal tar, and eight
ounces of emetic elixir* [to induce vomiting]. *This gave seven vomits and five
stools. After this, he was given five spoonfuls of sarsaparilla, and two ounces
of the laxative powder of sena. This purged very well. The third day there was
given three glasses of the white of hen's dung in white wine, along with sugar.
And so he was cured.*"

I closed the journal and tossed it onto the countertop.

"There, John—what do you think about that?"

He was staring at me, his mouth hanging open.

"I'd say his patients all got well," Amy interjected, a mischievous smile on her face. "He's got a better battin' average than you, Doc."

I snapped my head in her direction and cleared my throat.

Before I could say anything, she added, "Maybe you need to get you some hen's dung. Or at least some coal tar."

The good ole days
weren't always that good.

UNKNOWN

41

Spoiler Alert

Mamie Davenport was back from radiology, and the tech handed me the X-rays of her right hip. As I walked over to the view box, I knew what I was going to find. She was eighty-nine years old and had fallen this morning in her kitchen. Her right leg was shortened, her hip was extremely painful, and the X-rays only confirmed the diagnosis.

I walked over to room 4, clipboard in hand, and prepared to tell her about the surgery she would need to repair her broken hip.

The curtain had barely closed behind me when she spoke up and said, "Robert, we can talk about my hip in a minute. First, I want to tell you what happened in X-ray. So just sit down a minute, right in that chair."

She pointed to a stool by the side of her stretcher, and without hesitation I quickly obeyed.

Mamie and I had known each other for a long time. She and her late husband had been members of the church we joined when we moved to town, and Mamie had been one of our children's first and favorite Sunday school teachers. Up until this point, she had been living by herself at home, independent and self-sufficient. She was clear as a bell, and was quite a lady.

"Okay, Miss Mamie, what happened?"

In spite of her obvious pain, she managed a warm and genuine smile as she smoothed the sheet resting over her.

"Robert, you know if you just listen, you can learn something new every day," she told me, a twinkle in her eye.

"Hmm..." I responded, nodding and waiting for her to continue.

"While I was over in X-ray, these two cute little girls—I believe they're called 'radiology technicians'—started talking about some scary movie one of them had seen. She had apparently been watching it at a theater and become so frightened that she got up and walked out before it was over."

She paused and shook her head.

"I can't imagine paying good money and then simply walking out without seeing the whole film, can you?"

Before I could answer, she went on. "But apparently she did. And then later, when it came out on...what do you call it? BVDs or something?"

"*DVD,*" I gently corrected her.

"Right. Well, it seems she rented it and took it home to watch with her husband. Thought she could make it all the way through without getting too scared again. But before she would do that, she went to her computer and giggled it to—"

"She *googled* it?" I asked, trying hard not to laugh out loud.

"Giggled—googled. Just pay attention!"

I put a somber look on my face and sat up straight.

"Yes, Miss Mamie."

"Good," she responded. "Anyway, she wanted to know how the movie ended so she wouldn't get so scared this time. They were saying something about a *spoiler alert,* some kind of warning, making sure you don't spoil the ending by reading about it. But she wasn't about to watch that movie again without knowing what to expect."

I was really curious now. "What movie was it?"

She glanced over at me again, and with a look of mock sternness said, "It doesn't matter, and I don't remember, so just let me make my point."

When she was satisfied that I wasn't going to interrupt her again, she continued.

"She read the spoiler and knew exactly what was going to happen. She and her husband watched the whole movie, and even though it was really scary, they made it all the way through. Knowing the ending made it easier to watch."

Mamie was finished, and sat quietly looking over at me.

I was struggling with this, trying to understand what she was telling me.

Then in a calm, sure, and peaceful voice she said, "I know what you're going to say about my hip. It's broken, and I know what that means," she continued. "Not just the surgery part of it, but that I will probably never return to my home. And in fact, I may never leave this hospital. I know all about this. After all, I'm eighty-nine and the odds aren't with me."

She paused, and I just looked with wonder at this remarkable woman, trying to compose my next words. But just as she had done so many times in the past with my children and so many others, she was about to teach *me* something.

"But Robert, I've read the spoiler alert and I know what's going to happen. My story has already been written and it has a grand ending. I'm not afraid of what lies ahead—because you see, I will not be walking this path alone."

My hand was resting on the rail of her stretcher. She was smiling as she reached out and gently patted it.

"I'm not alone. Now, about my X-ray…"

My Father's will is that everyone who looks to the Son
and believes in him
shall have eternal life,
and I will raise them up at the last day.

JOHN 6:40

42

SOMETHING SPECIAL

Greater love has no one than this...

It was the day before Thanksgiving, and you would think the ER would be quiet. After all, there was last-minute shopping to be done for the big meal the following day, football was on television, and the weather was awful—rainy and cold. But so much for what should have been. The reality was that almost every bed was filled and three EMS units were out on runs. And it was only two o'clock in the afternoon.

Lori Davidson came out of triage, pushing an elderly woman in a wheelchair. They were closely followed by the woman's sister.

"Robert, we're so glad you're here today," the woman walking behind Lori said as they approached the nurses' station.

I recognized the voice and turned to look at Dorothy Myers, and then at Annie in the wheelchair.

"Fever and cough," Lori told me, nodding at Annie. "A little over 103."

I reached down and gently placed the back of my hand against her cheek. It was flushed and burning hot. She looked up and smiled at me when she felt my touch.

"Where are you taking her?" I asked Lori, glancing at the patient ID board and not seeing many options.

"Room 4 is open," she told me, pushing the wheelchair off in that direction. "I'll get her settled."

Dorothy stopped at my side and patted my arm. "So glad you're here," she said again.

Annie and Dorothy were both in their early eighties. I couldn't remember which was the older, but I thought it might be Annie. She had been born after a long and difficult labor, and hadn't breathed immediately after birth. A "blue baby," her parents had been told. The doctors hadn't seemed too concerned, but it soon became obvious that something wasn't right.

Annie wasn't developing normally, and she didn't seem to be responding to sights and sounds as you would expect. After several months and several doctors, they were given the devastating news that Annie had cerebral palsy. It looked quite severe, and she would never be normal.

The family rallied around Annie, and though the doctors had been right—she would never be able to walk and had a lot of trouble communicating—they included her in everything that went on. And when Dorothy was old enough, she became the caregiver for her older sister.

Over eight decades, that had never changed. Dorothy had become a schoolteacher and had never married. When their parents were no longer able to take care of Annie, she had moved in with Dorothy. And then when their parents were gone, they were the only family that the two of them had.

But that had been enough. Dorothy had always been involved with activities at her school, in the community, and in her church. And she had made sure that Annie went everywhere with her. And this afternoon, they were together once again in the ER.

Annie was in trouble. She was short of breath and her blood pressure was low. Her chest X-ray confirmed my fear—she had a significant pneumonia, with one lobe of her lungs completely socked in. She would need to be admitted to the hospital, and when Dorothy pulled me out into the hallway and pressed me for how many days this might take to resolve, I had to be honest with her.

"She might not be going home, Dorothy. She's eighty-three years old, weak, and really sick. I just don't know."

Dorothy took this news with the same quiet, calm demeanor she had always exhibited. Slowly nodding her head, she simply said, "I understand, Robert. I understand." And then she went back into Annie's room, pulled up a chair, and sat by her sister's side, as she had so many times for so many years.

At the nurses' station, I told Lori what we needed to do, and then asked our young secretary to get in touch with the pulmonary specialist on call.

Without looking up she said, "Hard to imagine taking care of a disabled person all of your life. I sure couldn't do it."

Lori had been writing on Annie's chart and immediately stopped. She put her pen down and looked over at the secretary.

"Janie, you're right. That *is* hard to imagine. But Dorothy is a special person. And…Annie is not *disabled*. She has *special needs*."

Her voice was firm, and Janie looked up, her eyes wide. Her lip was beginning to tremble and she seemed about to say something when Lori added, "And you know, we all have special needs, don't we?"

I looked over at Lori. There was no anger in her face or voice. She simply wanted Janie to understand this important lesson.

Then she smiled at her and said, "I just hope you have the chance to get to know Dorothy—to get to know both of them."

I glanced over at Annie's room. Dorothy still sat in her chair, gently stroking her sister's forehead and talking to her with peaceful and loving words. Annie was quietly looking up at her and smiling.

…than to lay down one's life for his friends.

JOHN 15:13 NKJV

THE REAL HEROES AMONG US

It was a Wednesday, three o'clock in the afternoon, and I thought the day would never end.

The ER had cranked up just after my shift had begun at seven a.m., and by noon we had seen a construction worker who had fallen fifteen feet from a scaffold, two cardiac arrests, an elderly woman with a fractured neck, and an assortment of other maladies. I was finishing up the chart of a nine-year-old with appendicitis, when Lori walked up to the nurses' station and put a chart in the "to be seen" stack.

She turned to me and was about to say something, when the unit secretary spoke up. "Dr. Lesslie, there're two ambulances coming in from a car-versus-truck accident out on Highway 21. Should be here in about fifteen minutes."

"Okay," I sighed. I glanced over at Lori but she was already heading back out to triage.

Fifteen minutes. That might give me enough time to see this next patient Lori had just brought back and put in room 2. I picked up the chart and read the chief complaint.

Cold, congestion, pulling on ears.

It was a one-year-old, and in the box marked "Family Physician" was the abbreviation "NFD" (No Family Doctor).

"Great," I sighed again, this time with a little frustration. This looked like something that could be taken care of in a clinic or doctor's office, and not the ER.

I headed to room 2 and glanced at the clock on the wall, marking the time and the expected arrival of our ambulance patients.

The curtain's rings rattled loudly as I pulled it aside and walked in. A young woman of twenty-five or so sat on the stretcher, holding an infant in her arms. She smiled as I walked over and put the chart on the countertop.

Standing at the head of the bed was a girl of about six years, her hair neatly French-braided, her dress less than new but clean and crisply ironed.

Her hand rested on the head of a young boy, probably three or four years old. It was her brother, and he looked up at me with the smiling, guileless eyes of a child with Down's syndrome. Without a word he walked over to where I stood and hugged my leg.

"That's Charlie," the young woman said. "He's fine, and I'm sorry, he's just never met a stranger."

She was reaching down to pull him away as I said, "No, that's fine." I stooped down and put my hand on his shoulder. "Charlie, I'm Dr. Lesslie," I told him. "I'm going to take a look at your little brother, if that's okay." My earlier frustration was rapidly melting away.

He nodded his head and pointed up to the infant.

"That's Andrew," he told me. "He's sick."

I stood up and turned back to the woman and the child in her arms. Glancing down at the chart again, I noted his vital signs. His temperature was a little elevated at 100, but everything else seemed fine.

"I think he has another ear infection," she told me, rocking the baby in her arms. He was cautiously looking up at me, and seemed alert and in no distress.

I asked her a few questions about Andrew and then examined him, in spite of some loud protestations on his part. He in fact had an ear infection and would need to be treated with antibiotics.

"Does he have a doctor?" I asked her.

"No, none of the children do," she answered, lowering her head a little. "We moved to Rock Hill a couple of months ago and haven't been able to find a doctor who will take new Medicaid patients."

It was a story we heard too often in the ER. I was about to say something, when she added, "I'm sorry we had to come to the emergency room. I know you're busy, but we had nowhere else to go. And Andrew can get really sick in a hurry. I just didn't—"

I was suddenly ashamed of my earlier reaction. This woman and her children had fallen through the cracks in the system and needed help.

"That's fine," I interrupted, sensing her discomfort. "That's why we're here. We'll give you the names of some doctors here in town who I think will see your children. And a nurse will be back in just a minute with some prescriptions for Andrew. We'll get him better."

I turned to the entrance and pulled the curtain aside.

"Thank you, Dr. Lesslie," she said quietly behind me.

"Thank you, Doctor," Charlie echoed.

I walked back to the nurses' station and had just enough time to write up Andrew's chart and fill out his prescriptions before sirens announced the ambulances' arrival. Flipping the chart over, I noticed that Lori had written "single mother, new in town, no family."

A few minutes later, while the paramedics were wheeling their stretchers into the department and toward the trauma room, I glanced out into the parking lot.

Andrew's mother was putting the last of her children safely into an old and battered Dodge van. I watched as she climbed in and cranked the stubborn engine. Thick, black smoked billowed from the exhaust pipe as she slowly pulled out of the parking lot and down the street.

This was a strong woman. One day her children would understand that—and would understand how fortunate they were to have her.

"Dr. Lesslie, we need you in major trauma!"

Her children arise and call her blessed.

PROVERBS 31:28

44

No Regrets

I think this is a friend of yours," Jeff Ryan, our triage nurse, said, sliding the chart of minor trauma, bed A, in front of me. "Got tangled up with a table saw and messed up a couple of his fingers. Nothing too bad, but he's going to need a little work."

He turned and headed back out to triage as I glanced down at the record.

Reid Townsend. 58 yr old male. Lacerations of left fingers.

He *was* a friend of mine. I picked up his clipboard and headed down the hallway to minor trauma.

I had known Reid since shortly after we had moved to Rock Hill. He was an executive with one of our local companies. We had met one night in the ER when he'd brought his father in with pneumonia. I had always appreciated his dry sense of humor and his relaxed demeanor. I hoped that Jeff was right and that his fingers were not too badly damaged.

Reid was the only person in the four-bed room. I walked over, pulled up a stool, and sat down beside him.

"What in the world have you done to yourself?" I asked him.

He shook his head and held up his towel-wrapped hand, now soaked in blood. Sheepishly he explained what had happened.

"Robert, it was really stupid. I have a small shop in the back of the garage, and I do a little woodworking now and then. I was working on a picture frame for my wife and I just got careless. I must have looked away from the table saw and *wham!* That blade grabbed my fingers and chewed 'em up pretty good. Funny, though—it didn't hurt for a while. Just bled a lot. But I'm starting to feel it now."

"Let's take a look," I said, taking his hand and carefully removing the makeshift bandage. "Want this?" I asked, holding up the towel.

"Are you kidding? No, you guys can have that thing. I just want my fingers."

The saw had been unforgiving, but the blade hadn't severed any tendons or reached any bones. It was a mess, but he wasn't going to lose anything.

Relieved to hear this, Reid settled back on his stretcher and let me do my work. It was going to take awhile, and we would have some time to talk.

"So," I said, turning his hand over to better visualize the lacerations. "Other than carving fingers, what have you been doing with yourself?"

"Not a whole lot, Robert," he answered quietly. "Not since my father died."

I stopped what I was doing and looked up at him.

"I didn't know," I responded. "When did that happen?"

Reid sighed and looked down at his wounded hand. "About a month ago," he answered. "He was ninety-seven years old, and it was time. He'd had a tough couple of years."

I nodded and resumed my work, waiting for him to say something else. When he didn't, I asked, "How has that been for you? Are you doing okay?"

Reid and his father, Jeremiah, had been very close. There were two other children, a son and a daughter, but Reid had been the main care-taker for as long as I had known him. Though Jeremiah was elderly and had been suffering with dementia, he was Reid's father, and I knew Reid must still be grieving.

He sighed quietly again, and softly said, "Mainly I'm tired. His last four or five months were especially hard on us, him and me. It was just the two of us, and he became more and more dependent on me. Some days he seemed clearer than others, and that's when I sensed his embar-rassment. He didn't want to be a burden. One day he told me just that and he started to cry."

His voice choked and he was silent for a while. Then he went on. "Other times, though, he just seemed happy that I was with him, and noth-ing bothered him. I was glad for those times."

We didn't say anything for a while. I continued piecing his fingers back together and he just watched.

After a few minutes I paused, needing to stretch my back. Sitting up straight on the stool, I rolled my shoulders and looked up at him.

"Any regrets?" I asked.

He chuckled and the familiar twinkle returned to his eyes.

"Robert, are you an ER doc or a psychiatrist?" he quipped.

"No psychiatrist," I answered. "But I've lost my father too, and there are some things I wish I had asked him, and some things I wish I had told him."

He slowly nodded his head, and with concern in his voice said, "I've thought a lot about that. Maybe everybody does. In my heart I know I did what I needed and wanted to do with my father. I chose to spend time with him, even when it wasn't convenient, and even when he seemed not to know me. Part of it was not wanting to be on this side of things and wishing I had done more. But I guess most of it was wanting to do the right thing while I still had the time. I'm just glad I had the chance to do it."

"You *made* the chance, Reid," I told him. "And you did the right thing. You'll soon get over being tired and you'll be fine, but the burden of regret doesn't easily go away. Sometimes it never does."

We looked at each other for a moment and then he laughed.

"Maybe you *are* a psychiatrist after all."

Of all sad words of tongue or pen,
the saddest are these: "It might have been!"

JOHN GREENLEAF WHITTIER (1807–1892)

45

Apples and Oranges

M rs. Loretta Kensington. The name struck terror into the hearts of everyone in the ER. And here she was again, being wheeled into the department by her grim and prim caregiver.

"My usual room, please," she directed Lori Davidson, pointing over to room 2. "I assume you have it ready for me."

Lori had been waiting at the nurses' station for Mrs. Kensington, making sure the room was kept unoccupied.

"Yes, Mrs. Kensington," she answered. "We've been expecting you."

Lori rolled her eyes in my direction, picked up the clipboard for room 2, and led the procession into the cubicle.

Loretta looked over at me, harrumphed, and gave me a curt nod as she was being wheeled away.

Loretta Kensington was in her seventies now, the widow of one of Rock Hill's leading businessmen. Mr. Kensington had owned one of the first banks in the area and had made a fortune, leaving it all to his wife. The couple had no children, and Loretta lived alone with her caregiver, Ms. Blackstone.

No one knew Ms. Blackstone's first name, or if she even had one. She never spoke, and she communicated with her employer through silent nods and shakes of her head. Her attire was unchanging—a drab gray dress, black leather shoes, and in cool weather, a yellowed lace shawl. Her salt-and-pepper hair was always neatly bobby-pinned in a tight ball on the back of her head.

This was quite in contrast to Mrs. Kensington. The dowager was at all times resplendent in a colorful dress, cloaked in the skin of some unfortunate animal, and heavily laden with assorted bangles and baubles.

This morning was no exception. The pair disappeared behind the curtain, and I saw Virginia Granger staring and shaking her head as they passed her office door.

Virginia had gone to the administrator on at least three occasions, trying to have Loretta's medical care rendered somewhere other than the ER. And each time he had stood firm, reminding her that Mrs. Kensington's husband had been a longtime supporter of the hospital before his untimely death, and had served on the board for a number of years. This was the least we could do for his widow.

No matter that her "critical medical care" was only the drawing of some blood work every two weeks. Her doctor felt it important to monitor some of her lab values, and Loretta insisted it be done on Saturday mornings.

"I have too much to do during the week to be bothered with this blood-letting," she had complained to him. "It must be done on a Saturday."

Since we were the only place open for such things, it fell to the ER to provide her this service. Her appreciation was underwhelming.

Virginia looked over at me, pointed vigorously at the closed curtain of room 2 and then at me.

I shook my head at her but she raised a hand in the air, spun around, and disappeared into her office.

Great.

It fell to me to greet and welcome Mrs. Kensington to the ER and make sure that her visit went well. I waited as long as I could, then walked slowly over to her room.

The lab tech was just finishing drawing her blood when I entered.

"You were a little rough, young lady," she scolded the blushing tech. "Next time send someone with more experience."

The young woman scurried silently out of the room, and I stepped over to Loretta's wheelchair. Ms. Blackstone stood stonelike behind her, studying my every move.

"Mrs. Kensington," I said as cheerfully as I could muster. "Good to see you this morning."

"So you say, Dr. Lesslie," she grumbled. "I see this place is still a mess."

She was glancing around the room, her lips pursed and face scowling. I followed her gaze but didn't see anything out of the ordinary. After all, this was an ER. And it looked pretty clean to me.

"I'll speak to the administrator about the paint," she added, tapping one of the walls with the end of her cane. "Needs some brighter colors here."

I was about to say something, when she said, "Come, Blackstone. Let's be off."

I had to step quickly out of the way to avoid being run over. The pair was out of the room and speeding toward the nurses' station with me struggling to keep up.

They turned the corner and were headed toward the ambulance entrance, when an elderly man walked out of the triage hallway. Lori Davidson was right behind him, and she immediately put her hand on his shoulder. He stopped, narrowly avoiding being struck by the wheelchair.

"Watch where you're going, sir!" she shouted at the man. Then she looked him over from head to feet, wrinkled her nose, and said, "Blackstone, home."

And they were gone.

The mood of the department tangibly lightened, and I walked over to the triage entrance.

"What happened to you this morning, Clarence?"

"Oh, nothin' bad, Doc, and I don't mean to be any trouble," he answered, a huge grin spreading across his worn and wrinkled face. "Just a splinter in my hand that I can't get out."

Clarence Green was well-known to the ER staff. He had suffered a heart attack a few years ago and had come in with barely a blood pressure and barely clinging to life. He was convinced we had saved him, and every few weeks he would show up with eggs from his coop or collard greens from his garden. We told him it wasn't necessary, especially when we learned that he didn't have a car and rode his bike five miles to get here. But he just gave us that big grin of his and didn't say anything.

"He was splitting some wood and got a splinter in his left palm," Lori explained.

Clarence held out his huge, calloused hand for me to see. At the base of his thumb was the end of a piece of wood about the size of a toothpick. It disappeared into the fleshy part of his hand.

"That's going to need to come out," I told him, releasing his hand.

"That's why I'm here, Doc," he said. "Got to get back home and get some firewood split. Winter's a-comin'."

I remembered EMS telling us about his house when they picked him up with his heart attack. It was clean and neat, and he had a phone and electricity, but no heat—just his wood-burning fireplace.

"I don't need nothin' fancy," he had told them.

"He'll be back in minor trauma, bed A," Lori told me as she guided him down the hallway.

"Thanks, ma'am," Clarence said quietly, bowing his head just a little. "And thanks, Doc."

Wisdom's instruction is to fear the LORD,
and humility comes before honor.

PROVERBS 15:33

46

His Best Friend

Rock Hill ER, this is EMS 2."

Lori Davidson stepped over to the EMS radio, pushed the button, and picked up a notepad.

"Go ahead, EMS 2. This is the ER."

"We're on the way in with a sixty-three-year-old man—hypothermia. And probably a fractured femur."

Lori wrote this down then looked over at me.

"Major trauma," I silently mouthed.

"Roger, EMS 2. Major trauma when you get here," she instructed them.

"Should be ten to twelve minutes," the radio crackled, then went silent.

"Sounded like Denton Roberts," Amy Connors said. "I bet he doesn't like being out in the cold, not after just gettin' over the flu."

"You're right," Lori agreed. "I bet none of the guys do."

It had been brutally cold for the past three weeks, with high temperatures barely reaching the mid-twenties. That was unusual for this part of the Carolinas, and coupled with one of the worst flu seasons in a decade, it was wreaking havoc in the community.

"How's the guy in 4 doing?" I asked Lori. He was another man who had come in with a dangerously low temperature. He had been found in a deserted warehouse with only a few blankets to cover him, with a core temperature of 90 degrees.

"His temp is up to 94," she told me. "And he's starting to talk a little. He told me he was hungry and wanted some soup," she added.

"That's a good sign," I said. "And maybe some soup would be a good idea. Amy?"

"I'm on it," she responded without looking up, already dialing the kitchen.

"Better get the warming blanket ready and some heated IV fluids," I told Lori.

The radio crackled again and Denton Roberts was asking for help.

"Rock Hill ER, this is EMS 2! Our patient went into V-tach, blood pressure around 60. Any further orders?"

This was tricky, and my own heart rate quickened. The man's low temperature had caused his heart to be irritable, and the movement of getting him onto the stretcher might have been just enough to trigger this rapid and deadly rhythm. But at least he had a blood pressure. That gave us some time.

"How far out are you?" I asked, taking the receiver from Lori.

"We're just down the street, Doc. Two minutes max," Denton answered.

We could hear the approaching ambulance sirens through the automatic doors.

"Make sure he has some oxygen going and we'll be waiting."

Shocking him now might make matters worse. The most important thing to do was warm him up.

"10-4, Doc," Denton responded. "We're pulling in."

I handed the receiver back to Lori and headed toward major trauma.

"Amy, we need the lab down here, and an EKG," I called over my shoulder.

"Anything else?" she asked.

"Yeah, a miracle."

Lori and I were waiting as the ambulance doors opened and Denton Roberts wheeled his patient down the hallway and into major.

"Any change?" I asked him.

The man on the stretcher had his eyes closed, and his mouth was open and slack.

"No, still in V-tach," Denton answered, pointing down to their monitor.

He was right. It was ventricular tachycardia, and if it didn't convert back to a normal rhythm, we would have to make it happen. The man's body wouldn't stand it for very long.

"Be careful when you move him over," I cautioned Denton and his partner. "Gently."

Lori had readied the warming blankets and the heated IV fluids. Within a few minutes our patient, Preston Gaithers, was resting comfortably on our stretcher, still shivering and barely responsive. But his blood pressure had improved and his color was better.

"Whoa, look at that!" Lori exclaimed, pointing at the cardiac monitor.

There was a flurry of activity on the screen, with sudden spikes and pauses, and then he was back in a regular rhythm—90 beats a minute.

I felt myself relax a little, yet I knew his V-tach could return at any moment. We needed to get his temperature up.

"91 degrees," Lori answered my thoughts. That was 3 degrees higher than when he had first come in.

"Good," I told her. "We're making progress."

I stepped closer to the stretcher and put my hand on the man's chest.

"Mr. Gaithers, can you hear me?"

No response.

"Mr. Gaithers, can you—"

His eyelids fluttered a little and his head turned in my direction. That was enough for now.

"You're doing fine," I told him. "I know your leg must be hurting, but we need to get you warmed up before we take care of that."

His head nodded, just a little.

His femur was obviously fractured and badly angulated, and we had placed the leg in as much traction as was safe for the moment. But right now his temperature was the critical factor.

The door opened and Denton Roberts walked in, still making notes on his EMS chart.

"How's he doin', Doc?"

"Better," I told him. "Temp's coming up and he's starting to respond."

"And he's out of V-tach," Denton noted, pointing to the monitor.

He walked around the stretcher and stood beside me.

"This fella is really lucky," he said quietly.

"Lucky" might not be my first choice of words here.

"What do you mean?" I asked him.

"Well, by all rights he should be dead."

"I agree," I told him.

"No, he should be *dead*," Denton repeated, this time with decided emphasis.

I turned and looked at the paramedic, waiting for his explanation.

"We got the call and were the first ones there," he began. "The front door was locked and there were no lights on, so we had to break the door down to get in."

"Wait a minute!" I interrupted. "Who made the call?"

"It was a neighbor, a little lady a lot older than Mr. Gaithers here. She came around from the back when we made the ruckus knocking in the door. She hadn't seen him in a couple of days, and there hadn't been any lights on, and she thought something must have happened to him. She looked in one of the back windows and thought she saw him lying on the floor, then went home and called 9-1-1. She went back to try to break in, but like I said, she's tiny. And we were there in about five minutes. That's when she came around the house."

"Wow, he *is* lucky," Lori whispered from across the stretcher.

"That's not the lucky part," Denton responded, shaking his head. "As soon as we got the door open, I stepped in. It was pitch-black in there, and freezing. No heat and no electricity. Then all of a sudden, out of nowhere comes this gigantic dog—a golden retriever, I think. Scared me to death! He jumps up and puts his paws on my shoulders—and then dang it if he doesn't lick me right in the mouth."

Lori chuckled at this. When Denton cut his eyes at her, she turned her head away.

"Anyway, that dog jumped down and ran to the back of the house. He stopped a couple of times and looked back at us, like he was sayin' 'Come on!' Well, when we got back to the kitchen, there was Mr. Gaithers lying on the floor, curled up like a baby. And then that dog...that dog curled up right against him. The man's arm sorta went up and plopped across the dog, like he was huggin' him. And Doc, that retriever looked up at us and his tail wagged a few times—and I swear he made a noise like he was tryin' to talk."

Lori turned back to Denton and said, "He saved this man's life. I wonder how long—"

"No way of knowing," Denton interjected. "The dog wouldn't tell us that part."

I looked down at Preston Gaithers and saw a smile on his face.

"Where's the dog now?" I asked, realizing it would still be freezing in the man's house.

"Out in the ambulance with Freddy," Denton answered. "Warm as can be."

I looked over at Lori.

His Best Friend   199

"Is Virginia Granger still here?" I asked her, wondering if our head nurse was still in the department.

"No, she left…"

Lori's face suddenly softened, and with a smile she turned to Denton. "Let's go get that dog."

Lord…
No one but you and I understand
what faithfulness is…
Do not let me die until, for them,
all danger is driven away.

From *The Prayer of the Dog*
by Carmen Bernos de Gasztold (1919–)

47

HARK!

How did we draw the short straws?"

Jeff Ryan put three more charts in the "to be seen" basket and slumped against the counter. There were more patients to be brought back through triage, but he needed to catch his breath. It had been a long and busy evening.

"I guess we're just lucky," I chuckled without humor. It was eight o'clock on Christmas Eve, and we should have been home with our families.

"Yeah, sure," he grumbled. "I guess somebody has to be here."

He glanced over at the patient ID board and my eyes followed his. There was only one bed open in the entire department, and that was major trauma. We needed to keep it available for a significant or life-threatening problem.

Not that we didn't have "significant" patients already. I looked down at the ID square for minor trauma: there was a GSW (gunshot wound), a stab to the abdomen, and a burn to the shoulder. And there was the OD patient in GYN whom I hadn't seen yet.

I sighed and picked up the chart of my next patient. It was the twenty-three-year-old overdose.

Must not be very serious if they put him in GYN.

I walked down the hallway and ducked into minor trauma. I needed to check on the patients there.

The room was crowded, with every stretcher filled and two OR crews readying their patients to take around the corner to surgery.

The stab wound in bed B was stable now, with a huge gauze bandage wrapped around his abdomen. He had been in a poker game somewhere in town and, according to the investigating officer, it seems he had very sticky fingers. Or at least the person with the hawkbill knife thought so. Our patient had stumbled through the ambulance entrance holding his belly and calling for help. When one of our nurses had walked over and asked what his problem was, he had looked down and dropped his hands to his side. The nurse had screamed as part of his small intestines unraveled and almost hit the floor.

He was lucky. The curved blade hadn't hit any major vessels, and it looked like it had only nicked a small piece of bowel. "Stuff-stuff here" and "snip-snip there" and he would be fine.

The GSW was not as fortunate. He had been involved in a Christmas Eve drug deal gone bad. Two .22-caliber bullets had penetrated his large colon and left kidney. He should live also, but it would be a difficult couple of weeks for this eighteen-year-old young man.

"We'll be heading out in just a minute," one of the OR techs called out to me. "You don't have any more business for us, do you?"

I glanced up at the clock at the wall behind me, then back to the tech. "Not yet, but it's early."

The "burned shoulder" in bed C was having the wound cleaned and dressed. Another holiday argument, this one with his girlfriend. Probably ex-girlfriend by now. She had reportedly caught him with another woman—some mistletoe may have been involved—and a fight ensued. Unfortunately for our patient, there was some hot water boiling on a nearby stove and it quickly became a weapon. He would survive as well, but the scar would forever serve as a reminder of this Christmas Eve.

"I've written a prescription for some pain medicine," I told him. "And you need to follow up with your family doctor in two days."

He grumbled something, the nurse standing behind him shook her head, and I walked out of the room.

I looked down at the clipboard for the GYN room before entering: "Josh McKinney—OD—aspirin."

Interesting. I wonder if he knows he's in the gynecology room.

Josh was sitting in a chair in the corner of the room, still in his street clothes. He looked up as I closed the door behind me.

"Mr. McKinney, tell me about this overdose," I asked, stepping over and leaning against the exam table.

"It wasn't very much, Doctor, really," he said quietly. "Maybe five tablets. Six at the most. I don't even know why I did it."

His vital signs were normal and he wasn't in any distress. Still, I needed to know about any other medication, any alcohol, and whether he had any intention or plan of hurting himself.

We talked for a while, and it turned out that Josh knew one of my daughters. They had been in high school together before Josh had left for

Clemson. Two years and only a few credit hours later, he had dropped out and come home. His parents had become impatient with his lack of finding a job or returning to school and had kicked him out a few months earlier.

"This is my first Christmas away from home," he sighed. "My folks don't want any part of me."

I studied the young man for a moment. He looked up at me then hung his head and began wringing his hands.

"Do you know that for sure?" I asked him. "Do they know you're here?"

"They don't care," he said flatly. "Not anymore."

We sat there in silence for a few moments. It was Christmas Eve, and I couldn't let this pass.

"Josh, I'm going to try to get in touch with your parents and let them know you're here."

I waited for a response, but he just sat there, wringing his hands. That was answer enough for me.

"Susie," I said to the unit secretary, sliding Josh's chart to her, "could you try to get in touch with this boy's parents? Just let me know."

"Ho! Ho! Ho!"

We all looked over to the ambulance entrance and stared in amazement as Virginia Granger walked in, dressed in civilian clothes. Most of the staff had never seen her in anything other than her immaculately starched white uniform.

"Merry Christmas!" she called out to the department.

"Have you been into the eggnog?" Jeff bravely asked, walking up and intently surveying his head nurse.

"Hardly," she chuckled, but she eyed him sternly. "Just got out of the candlelight service at our church and thought I'd pay you all a visit. Here."

In her hands was a huge platter of Christmas cookies. I could see multicolored sugar cookies, brownies—and ladyfingers, looking just the way my mother had made them.

"Looks like you guys could use some cheer," she added, glancing around the crowded department.

"Thanks, Ms. Granger," Jeff told her, taking the platter and heading toward the lounge.

"Save some for me!" I called after him.

"Robert, come here a minute," Virginia said, motioning to the medicine room.

We walked in and she reached into her large purse, fished around in it, then pulled out what appeared to be a church bulletin.

"This is the program from tonight's service at the church. Now I don't know about you, but I've been singing Christmas carols for a lot of years, and most times I just seem to go through the motions. I really don't pay a lot of attention to the words or their meaning. They're just so familiar, I guess. But tonight I did pay attention, and when we were singing 'Hark, the Herald Angels Sing' and came to the last verse, something struck me."

I thought her voice might be trembling as she said this last part, and I studied her face. Her eyes were moist and reddened, and she was looking straight at me.

"Something told me you all, maybe just *you*, needed to read this."

She handed me the folded bulletin and pointed to the last verse of the carol. With a black pen she had underlined parts of it.

> *Hail the heav'n-born <u>Prince of Peace</u>!*
> *Hail the Sun of Righteousness!*
> *Light and life to all He brings,*
> *Ris'n <u>with healing in his wings</u>.*
> *Mild He lays His glory by,*
> *Born that man no more may die;*
> *Born to raise the sons of earth;*
> *Born to give them second birth.*
> *Hark! The herald angels <u>sing</u>,*
> *"Glory to the newborn King!"*

I read through the verse a second time, slower, paying attention to every word. Then I looked up at Virginia. Her eyes were dry now, and she was smiling.

"And Robert, the angels are *still* singing."

We just looked at each other.

"Dr. Lesslie."

It was Susie, calling to me from the nurses' station and holding up the phone.

"Mr. McKinney for you. He's the father of the young man back in GYN."

48

DAN QUIGLEY

I s that it, Doc?" my patient asked me, holding up his thumb. "Is that all I'm going to feel?"

I had just given an anesthetic block to both sides of the digit, and in another minute or two he wouldn't be feeling anything.

"That's all there is to it," I told him, turning on my stool and organizing the surgical repair kit on the stand beside me. The man had cut his thumb on a lawn-mower blade and was going to need a few stitches.

"Wow, that wasn't so bad," he said. "Nothin' to it."

We were back in the four-bed minor-surgery room in the ER at the old Greenville General Hospital. I was an intern rotating through the department, and I was spending the evening putting people back together. It turned out to be a bad night for fingers and thumbs. The triage nurse had just put a patient in the stretcher beside us and pulled the curtain closed for privacy. I caught a glimpse of a middle-aged man's frightened, pasty face and the blood-soaked rag around one of his fingers. That would be my next case, unless one of the other docs on duty picked up the chart.

As I was suturing the injured thumb, I heard some familiar whistling in the hallway. And then Dan Quigley walked into the room.

Dan was an interesting guy. He gave us a lot of smiles. A third-year family-practice resident, he was spending the last month of his residency in the ER. He was of medium height, slender, and almost completely bald, with only wisps of light brown hair encircling his shiny head. His demeanor was that of a college professor. He was very intense, focused, and took himself and everything he dealt with very seriously.

"Good evening, Robert," he said, walking over and standing behind me. He had a clipboard in his hand, and he drummed it rhythmically with his fingers. "Whatcha got there?"

He peered over my shoulder and moved his head from side to side.

"Hmmm," he murmured with an uncomfortable seriousness.

I glanced up at my patient and watched as his eyes widened. He first looked up at Dan, then back to his thumb, and then again to Dan.

"Good luck with that one," he said with finality, then turned and stepped behind the curtain beside us.

I leaned close to my patient and whispered, "Don't worry. I don't think he even works here."

The man's eyes widened even more and I thought he might bolt.

"Just kidding," I whispered again. "You're going to be fine."

From behind the curtain, we both heard the "hmmm" again, this time more prolonged and much graver.

Then Dan spoke to his patient in a kind and calming voice.

"This is a bad laceration, and you should feel fortunate that I'm on duty in the ER tonight. I think I'm going to be able to save your finger."

There was a muffled gasp from behind the curtain. "But what—"

"Don't you worry," Dan comforted him. "Let me get my special instruments and we'll start to work. I'm not going to let you lose that finger."

As he walked out of the room he glanced over in my direction and with a grave look on his face, nodded at me. I immediately rolled back and peered around the corner of the curtain.

Dan's patient was sitting bolt upright. His mouth was hanging open and his wide and frightened eyes were staring at his left index finger. There was a half-inch laceration down one side, and it wasn't very deep. Two, maybe three stitches tops.

He looked over at me and didn't say anything. I pursed my lips and shook my head.

"You're going to be fine," I said quietly. "It's nothing bad, and you're not going to lose anything."

He settled back on the stretcher and took a deep breath, exhaling slowly. But he didn't stop staring at his finger.

I turned back to my own patient and finished sewing up his wound. Somehow we had managed to save his finger.

"This is a wild place, Doc," he told me as he was leaving. "A wild place."

He was right. But it wasn't as wild as one morning in the pediatric clinic with Dan Quigley.

Dan hadn't always been bald. Sometime during the summer of his first year in residency he had miraculously gained a full head of hair. Rumor had it that he was employing a quite new technique—first, a strip of Velcro was glued to the top of the wearer's head, and then a well-tailored toupee was pressed into place on top of the strip. Dan had missed a little on the "well-tailored" part—the edges of the brown wig barely reached his own remaining hair, which was now a mixed salt-and-pepper. Yet it seemed to have added a spring to his step and made his bearing more upright. No one said anything to him about it, and after a while it became accepted and we forgot about it—until one morning in the pediatric clinic.

"Yo-aww!"

Someone had screamed behind the curtained opening of exam room 2. It sounded like Dan Quigley. He had just gone in to examine a three-year-old with asthma. Suddenly there followed the frightened wail of a young child and a young woman's strident admonition to "Put that thing down, Johnny!"

Dan burst through the curtain, holding a clipboard in one hand and trying desperately to reposition his toupee with the other. He wasn't having much success. It was on sideways and hanging down over his eyes. His young patient had apparently been intrigued by whatever was clinging to the doctor's head and had reached up and grabbed it. It must have been difficult to know who had been the most surprised when it came off.

Dan stormed past us, tossed the clipboard down on the counter, and slammed the door of the doctor's office behind him. A few minutes later, he emerged smiling, toupee in place, and with a look in his eye that dared any of us to say anything.

That should have changed his mind about wearing a toupee, but it took Moose Matthews to finally convince him.

Moose was also a family practice resident, a year behind Dan. He was a big man and a big hunter—deer, turkey, dove, ducks—anything that was legal and in season, and some that weren't. Monday-morning rounds always brought stories of his weekend exploits.

The middle of the flu season found Moose, Dan, and me taking calls for pediatrics. I was the intern on duty, and Dan was the senior resident. One particular day had been extremely busy and we didn't make it to the call room until three in the morning. We all had bunks and were soon tucked in, hoping for a little sleep. Moose was up for the next call, and the phone was on the table beside his bed.

I had just dozed off when the telephone rang. There was some rummaging around from the general direction of Moose's bunk as he struggled in the dark to find the phone.

"What the—! Arghhh!"

The yell was blood-curdling, and I bolted upright in my bed, startled and confused in the complete darkness.

It was Moose, and he kept on yelling. Then I heard him stumble out of his bed and stomp around the room, bumping into furniture and almost falling across me.

"Arghhh!"

Suddenly the lights came on, and there stood Moose right in front of me. There was a wild look in his eyes, and his arms were thrashing around in the air, just inches from my face. He almost hit me with the furry thing in his hand—Dan's toupee!

Dan's finger was still on the light switch when I glanced over at him. We hadn't realized he had taken off his toupee and tossed it over on the table. Then the phone had rung.

Without saying a word, Dan got out of bed and walked over to Moose. The fearless hunter stood motionless, wearing only his drawers and staring down at the "thing" in his hand. He reached out and handed it to Dan.

The phone was still ringing.

"It's your turn," Quigley told Moose. He climbed back into bed and pulled the sheet over his head. And that was the last we saw of the toupee.

Dan's gone now. But whenever I think of him, I remember that night, and I smile.

That of all days is the most completely wasted
in which one did not once laugh.

CHAMFORT (1741–1794)

49

CHARLIE WHITE

Gary Neal was headed for big trouble. He was only seventeen, but he already had a reputation—and an extensive rap sheet—with the city police.

"This kid is bad news," Officer Blake told me as we stood together at the nurses' station. "How long before you get him put back together?"

He was pointing down to the chart in front of me, referring to the young man back in the minor trauma room.

Gary had been brought into the ER in handcuffs, having been on the losing end of a fight somewhere downtown. The gash on the side of his head would take fifteen or twenty stitches to repair, and about an hour to finish.

When I explained that to Blake, his partner, Sergeant Charlie White, asked if he could go talk to the patient for a minute. I was still writing up the record so I told him that would be fine.

White headed down the hallway to minor trauma, and I turned to Blake.

"What do you think that's about?" I asked him.

"Sometimes Charlie's just a big mother hen," he answered. "Thinks he can save some of these kids—keep them from ending up in the big house in Columbia. He's always doing things with them on his days off, trying to keep them out of trouble. But not this one. Gary Neal is hard-core. Don't think I've seen anyone as pure mean as that boy."

I stopped writing and looked past Blake, down the hallway to the doorway of minor trauma.

"Why do you say that?" I asked him, curious. I had seen Gary plenty of times in the ER but didn't know much about his background. He was usually with the police and not in a very talkative mood.

"He's just flat-out mean," Blake repeated, shaking his head. "Can't say I blame him, though, after what he's been through. His father was just as mean, maybe more so, and left town when Gary was around two. His mother is—was—a druggie. OD'd on crack when the kid was about six, and he's been livin' with his aunt and uncle. They've tried, I guess, but he's been in trouble ever since. Just a matter of time before he really steps in it and gets put away."

"What do you think Charlie is saying to him?" I asked Blake.

"Probably what he always does," he answered, shaking his head. "He tries to convince these kids they're not worthless, that people care about them, and then he always tells them about Jesus. Charlie's a no-nonsense guy and doesn't mince his words. He makes it plain that the choices they're making are taking them down a dead-end street. I don't think they listen, though. None of them."

Blake stopped and took a deep breath.

"But he keeps trying," he said quietly.

Back in minor, I pulled up a stool beside Gary's stretcher and began repairing his laceration. He didn't say much, just an occasional "Oww!" or "How much longer?" But I noticed that every once in a while, he would glance over to the doorway where Sergeant White stood, and he would just look at the police officer. When Charlie would glance in Gary's direction, the boy would quickly look away.

It took just under an hour to sew him up, and then they were gone.

Years passed, and I forgot about Gary Neal and that night.

Then one afternoon, a man came into the department, his shirt and hands covered in blood. He looked around the department and his eyes settled on me. Quickly he walked over to where I stood.

"Remember me, Doc?" the man asked.

The name was familiar, and I studied his face, trying without success to place him.

He was carrying a little boy in his arms—his three-year-old son, as it turned out. The boy had fallen off a swing and busted his left eyebrow. There was a lot of blood, but it wasn't a serious injury.

"I used to come visit you a lot," he chuckled. "Gary Neal." And then I remembered.

But this was a different person. He was clean-cut, self-assured, and smiling. This wasn't the lost seventeen-year-old I had known.

He told me about his life, about his decision to change things, about going to college and becoming an engineer—and especially about the night in jail when he had gotten down on his knees with Charlie White and prayed.

"That's when things began to turn around," he said quietly. "The *Lord* changed my life, but the Sarge led me to him."

We were back in minor trauma, and he was sitting with his son on one of the corner stretchers.

"And it all started right here, in this room," he said, glancing around the small space. "This is where I began to see a different path."

A farmer went out to sow his seed...
Some fell along the path...Some fell on rocky places...
Other seed fell among thorns...
Still other seed fell on good soil, where
it produced a crop—
A hundred, sixty, or thirty times what was sown.

JESUS, IN MATTHEW 13:3-9

50

Emma

Not many people knew her last name. But you really didn't need to. All you had to do was say "Emma," and everyone in town immediately knew who you were talking about.

I first met her in the ER more than fifteen years ago. She hadn't been a patient, but had come in with a friend of hers, an elderly woman with a serious pneumonia. I can still see her standing at the head of the woman's stretcher, gently stroking her hair and quietly speaking words of encouragement. Then she had taken a pad of paper out of her purse and begun making notes. First she was jotting down the things I was saying, and later she made a list of what her friend would need while she was in the hospital. There were family members and friends to be called, cats to be taken care of, cleaning to be done, and so on. All the while Emma had a smile on her face.

A few years later, she came in with her own emergency. It was her first heart attack, and it was all we could do to convince her she needed to stay in the hospital.

"I don't want to be a burden," she had repeatedly insisted. "And I've got so much to do, and people who depend on me."

She quickly recovered but continued to have heart problems, with two more attacks over the next couple of years.

When Emma died a few days ago, there was no family to provide details about her life—when she was born, where she was born, next of kin. It was as if she had simply passed through this life and disappeared, without leaving a trace.

But that description would be far from reality. This remarkable woman had in fact left quite a trace.

You might not have known that unless you were at Barrett's Funeral Home last night for her visitation. That in itself was a little unusual, since there were no family members to stand in a greeting line, shaking hands and exchanging heartfelt condolences. It seems that some anonymous individual had placed a notice in the local paper about her death and then arranged for everything at Barrett's. The note had been brief, simple, and to the point:

Emma—October 5, 2011
Visitation at Barrett's
7-9 p.m., October 7

You wouldn't think that many people would notice such a small thing, but by seven-thirty the whole funeral home was full and people were standing around outside the front doors. There was a little confusion when folks first arrived. There was no receiving line and no one really giving directions. You just walked in and sort of started milling around, looking for someone you knew.

Before long, there were clusters of people standing together, talking and sharing their stories about the woman they had all come to honor.

It was a peculiar gathering. In one corner of the main lobby was the city mayor, surrounded by some of the leading businesspeople of the area. Each of them had something to say about Emma, about the time she had appeared in their office with something she had baked and a kind word—and usually the request to help someone who was down on their luck or in a jam of some sort.

And there was the police captain with some of his officers. Emma had been no stranger to the inmates in the city jail.

"She's been visitin' the detention center for longer than I can remember," he had said. "And no matter how rowdy those guys were, whenever they saw Miss Emma comin', it was always 'Yes, ma'am' and 'No, ma'am.' I remember one Christmas Eve…"

Not too far from these uniformed gentlemen stood a group of poorly dressed individuals. They were quietly talking among themselves, frequently casting suspicious glances at the nearby officers, clearly uncomfortable with the proximity of these representatives of the law. But they had stories to share as well: about the time Emma had paid an electric bill, keeping the power on during the coldest February in fifty years—or the summer she had brought a box of clothes for their children, right out of the clear blue. How had she known to do that?

The stories went on and on, and the conversations became louder and more animated. This was a celebration, an act of thanksgiving for a woman who had touched and changed so many lives. A woman whose last name they didn't even know.

Unobserved by this crowd, sitting against a wall in one of the far corners, was an elderly gentleman, obviously deep in quiet and somber thought. He was studying a piece of paper held in his gnarled and time-worn hands. Slowly he stood and stepped out into the middle of the room.

He stood there, not saying anything, and the people around him turned and hushed. The silence spread like a breeze throughout the building, and people began pressing into the cramped space to see what was going on. No one spoke a word.

It was the old man who finally broke the suspended calm.

"The last couple of years, when Emma couldn't see well enough to drive, I would take her where she needed to go," he began. His voice was cracking, but there were no tears in eyes—just the beginning of a smile at the corners of his mouth.

"Last week, I think she knew she didn't have much longer on this earth, and she gave me this piece of paper." He paused and held up the wrinkled sheet of typing paper. "She wanted me to have it, but I think she'd want you to hear it too. So I'm going to read it. There is one place she under-lined a couple of times, so it must have been important to her. I'm going to repeat that part, 'cause I need to remember it."

Then in the holy silence of that place, he read what she had long ago typed out on the paper, a quote from the Quaker William Penn.

I expect to pass through life but once.
If therefore, there be any kindness I can show,
or any good thing I can do to any fellow being,
<u>let me do it now</u>,
and not defer or neglect it,
as I shall not pass this way again.

Let me do it now.

And what does the Lord require of you?
To act justly and to love mercy
and to walk humbly with your God.

Micah 7:8

Let me do it now.

Notes

Page 15: "Jesus sought me when a stranger..." words by Robert Robinson (1735–1790).

Page 204: "Hail the heav'n-born Prince of Peace!..." words by Charles Wesley (1707–1788), arr. William H. Cummings (1831–1915).

D r. Robert Lesslie, bestselling author of *Angels in the ER, Angels on Call,* and *Angels and Heroes,* is a physician who lives and actively practices medicine in Rock Hill, South Carolina. Board-certified in both emergency medicine and occupational medicine, he is the co-owner of two busy urgent care/occupational clinics.

For more than 25 years, Dr. Lesslie worked in and directed several of the busiest ERs in the Charlotte, North Carolina, area. He also served as medical director of the emergency department at Rock Hill General Hospital for almost 15 years. During his tenure as medical director, he received the American Medical Association's Continuing Education Award. He also traveled around the country, giving lively, innovative lectures to the Emergency Nurses Association at their annual meetings in major cities.

For seven years, Dr. Lesslie wrote a weekly medical column for *The Charlotte Observer* presenting a wide variety of topics, both medical and editorial. He also pens a regular column on medical, philosophical, and personal topics for the *YC,* a monthly publication in York County, North Carolina.

Dr. Lesslie enjoys the fast-paced environment of the ER and the need to make rapid and accurate diagnoses. He views his medical career as an opportunity to go beyond simply diagnosing and treating individual patients. For him, it is a way to fulfill a higher calling by meeting the real physical and emotional needs of his patients.

An active member of his home church in Rock Hill, Dr. Lesslie serves as an elder, and he and his wife, Barbara, teach Sunday school and sing in the church choir. They are also involved with an outreach program for disabled/handicapped individuals, Camp Joy, where Dr. Lesslie serves as the camp physician for a week each summer. He also enjoys mentoring high-school and college students considering a career in medicine.

Dr. Lesslie and his wife, Barbara, have been married for more than 35 years. Together they have raised four children—Lori, Amy, Robbie, and Jeffrey—and are now enjoying five grandchildren. In his spare time, Dr. Lesslie enjoys gardening, golf, hunting, reading, and bagpiping.

www.robertlesslie.com

Also by Robert Lesslie, MD

Angels in the ER
Inspiring True Stories from an Emergency Room
Doctor

*If you don't believe in angels…*you should spend
some time in the ER. You'll learn that angels do exist.
Some are nurses, a few are doctors, and many are every-
day people:

* …such as well-starched head nurse Virginia
  Granger, whose heart of compassion hides
  behind a steely gaze.

* …or William Purvis—a.k.a. "Max Bruiser"—a
  beefy pro wrestler who has a tussle with an unexpected opponent.

* …Or Macey Love, whose determination to love her two granddaugh-
  ters—and everyone else she meets—is expressed in just the radiance
  of her smile.

In this bestselling book of true stories—some thoughtful, some delightful,
some heart-pumping—you'll see close-up the joys and struggles of people like
you. Along with them, you can search your own heart for answers to finding grace
and peace in the darkness, and living well in the light.

Angels on Call
Inspiring True Stories from the ER

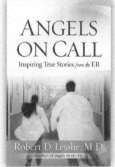

Dr. Robert Lesslie shares experiences—some heart-
warming, some edge-of-your-seat—that reveal answers
to those often unspoken pleas of "Who can I turn to?"
"Who's on call for me?"

* …Sally Carlton and Wanda Bennett are both in
  desperate situations. But sometimes the passion
  for life burns where least expected.

* …Wesley Wood is rushed through the doors on
  a stretcher, undergoing CPR from a 300-pound
  nursing attendant sitting on his chest. He clearly needs some help—
  but how?

Throughout these remarkable accounts, you'll also catch glimpses of those
who are now asking, "Who am I on call *for*?" It is these people who have found
the kind of healing we all need.

Angels and Heroes
True Stories from the Front Line

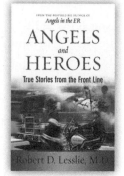

Every day, courageous men and women from the police, fire, and EMS face danger with the grace and strength of angels. Dr. Robert Lesslie gives you a new appreciation of their amazing experiences as he takes you close-up to...

* breathtaking moments from the front lines of the police

* heart-pounding incidents with firemen

* poignant accounts from the men and women of EMS

* and unforgettable heart-and-soul rescues from the ER

In these remarkable true stories you'll see the human connections and the divine moments of the heroes among us...and be encouraged to watch for those times when you too might be able to rescue someone with God's love and care.

Angels on the Night Shift
Inspirational True Stories from the ER

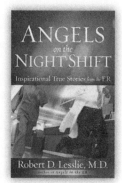

During the darkest hours of the night—and our lives—we need someone to comfort us and help us endure. Sometimes a nurse, a doctor, another patient, even a stranger is the "angel" who sees us through till the sun rises again.

In these remarkable glimpses into the heart of the ER, Dr. Robert Lesslie opens the curtain on the fears, hopes, conflicts, and resolutions that go on even as illnesses are treated, lives are saved, and griefs are dealt with. You will gain a window on some of life's greatest wonders and mysteries while you share the joys and struggles, the failures and redemptions, of people just like you.

Ordered

The Story of Your Life
Inspiring Stories of God at Work in People Just like You

Matthew West and Angela Thomas

When Grammy-nominated recording artist Matthew West invited people to share their stories, he received nearly 10,000 responses. As he read every one, entering into other people's joy, pain, and hope in God, his heart was transformed.

In *The Story of Your Life*, Matthew and fellow author Angela Thomas respond to 52 of those stories, considering what God is doing in each situation. You'll read about...

- Wendy, the unmarried girl who gives birth to her daughter in jail, and how God turns her life around

- Kristen, the foster girl who is about to turn 18 and has nowhere to go, and how she discovers that God is her true Father

- Greg, the pastor whose congregation lines the streets with banners and cheers when he and his wife bring home Lily, the little girl they adopt from Guatemala

In these inspiring glimpses into people's lives, you'll see how God is at work in everyone's story—including yours.

Four Paws from Heaven
Devotions for Dog Lovers

M.R. Wells, Kris Young, and Connie Fleishauer

Friend, family member, guardian, comforter—a dog can add so much to our lives. These furry, four-footed creatures truly are wonderful gifts from a loving Creator to bring joy, laughter, and warmth to our hearts and homes. These delightful devotions will make you smile and perhaps grow a little misty as you enjoy true stories of how God watches over and provides for us even as we care for our canine companions.

Heavenly Horse Sense
Inspirational Stories from Life in the Saddle

Rebecca E. Ondov

Horsewoman and bestselling author Rebecca Ondov invites you on some amazing horseback pack trips in Montana's Bob Marshall Wilderness. Drawing on 15 years of working from the saddle, she takes you into the mountains to discover the unique personalities of horses and mules, the beauty of God's creation, and the wonders—and dangers—of nature. You'll experience...

- three miracles in the life of a foal named Rahab
- the ingenuity of a mule that reveals a strategy for handling trouble
- a newborn filly's playfulness, which demonstrates God's desire for relationship

Along the trail you'll encounter the amazing love and wisdom God offers if you'll only ask.